100**FUNK**GROOVES
FORELECTRIC**BASS**

Learn 100 Bass Guitar Riffs & Licks in the Style of the Funk Legends

DAN**HAWKINS**

FUNDAMENTAL**CHANGES**

100 Funk Grooves for Electric Bass

Learn 100 Bass Guitar Riffs & Licks in the Style of the Funk Legends

ISBN: 978-1-78933-217-9

Published by **www.fundamental-changes.com**

Copyright © 2020 Dan Hawkins

www.fundamental-changes.com

Over 11,000 fans on Facebook: **FundamentalChangesInGuitar**

Instagram: **FundamentalChanges**

For over 350 Free Guitar Lessons with Videos Check Out

www.fundamental-changes.com

Cover Image Copyright: Shutterstock, Sergey Nivens

Contents

Introduction

Funk has probably influenced my style more than any other music, and I know this is also true for many other bass players. There's so much the instrument owes to masters like Larry Graham, Bootsy Collins and Marcus Miller. Funk arrived in the early '60s and never went away. Plus, everyone knows how important the bass is in funk music, which is something that can't be said for every genre!

In this book, each chapter features an introduction to a Funk sub-genre, followed by a gear checklist and recommended listening before getting to the grooves. There's even a Spotify playlist for you to dive into! Listen to as much different Funk as you can. That way, the music will start to permeate into your soul and eventually into your playing. Just scan the QR code below with your phone to get started.

Every bassline has an audio track, so you can hear how it should sound, plus there is a live recorded drumbeat to practice to. There are also plenty of backing tracks to keep you jamming! The live drumbeats are a fantastic resource and will help you to build your groove, feel, and timing – essential in funk bass playing.

Always keep in the groove and use your ear to play what you hear in your head.

Enjoy!

Dan

Get the Spotify playlist to accompany this book now by scanning the QR code

Get the Audio

The audio files for this book are available to download for free from **www.fundamental-changes.com.** The link is in the top right-hand corner. Simply select this book title from the drop-down menu and follow the instructions to get the audio.

We recommend that you download the files directly to your computer, not to your tablet, and extract them there before adding them to your media library. You can then put them on your tablet, iPod or burn them to CD. On the download page there is a help PDF and we also provide technical support via the contact form.

For over 350 Free Guitar Lessons with Videos Check out:

www.fundamental-changes.com

Over 11,000 fans on Facebook: **FundamentalChangesInGuitar**

Instagram: **FundamentalChanges**

Get the Video

Watch author Dan Hawkins break down some of the trickier techniques in this book and demonstrate them, step by step, in the bonus videos. Visit the Fundamental Changes website:

https://www.fundamental-changes.com/100-funk-grooves-for-electric-bass-bonus-videos/

Short link:

https://geni.us/funkvideos

Or scan the QR code with your smartphone:

Chapter One – Early Funk

The players: Bootsy Collins; Larry Graham

Despite being called *the Godfather of Soul*, it was James Brown who pioneered all forms of Funk. He was already established as a Rhythm & Blues and Soul artist when he started experimenting with more rhythmic music in the mid-sixties. Bass and drums were integral to his main musical aim of getting people gyrating, and *Cold Sweat* was the first presentation to the world of this energetic new genre.

His discovery of, and collaboration with, William Earl "Bootsy" Collins and his band The Pacemakers led to some of the most exciting and intense music of the last century. Bootsy was still in his teens when he played on classics like *Super Bad* and *Get Up (I Feel Like Being A) Sex Machine*.

Soul, R&B and Motown rhythms had until then emphasised the *backbeat* (beats two and four) and one of Brown's major innovations was to use beat one as the groove's focus. The whole band became a drum machine with horn stabs, pulsing basslines, percussive vocals and sometimes even two drummers playing at the same time. It was the bass, however, that became the bedrock and no longer hid away in the background.

The shockwaves from this new music reached all corners of the globe and permeated many sub genres. However, it was on the west coast of America that a talented group of musicians decided they wanted in on this new sound. Sly & The Family Stone were one of the first major groups in the US to incorporate both male and female, and white and black musicians. Their bass player, Larry Graham, was another titan of the instrument who used to play in hotels with his mum on lead vocals. When she decided to axe the drummer, he needed to provide more rhythm and suddenly the famous slap bass technique was born.

Without Funk, arguably there would be no Hip Hop, and George Clinton was another American musician who had a huge bearing on the music of the 1970s, '80s, and beyond. His music included references to psychedelia, humour, garish fashion and theatre. He was a prolific writer with many musical vehicles including Parliament and Funkadelic, and Bootsy Collins was involved in several of his early albums.

Both Bootsy Collins and Larry Graham would go on to feature in countless collaborations and solo projects, all in the name of Funk. Both these guys wanted to be seen and heard. They were responsible for bringing bass players directly into the public's consciousness.

Gear checklist: Bootsy is famous for his bright clothes and his Space Bass – a star-shaped instrument originally built by Washburn but currently made by Warwick. Despite the eye-catching shape, it features two single coil pickups and is really just a Fender Jazz bass in disguise. In fact, a late '60s Sunburst Fender Jazz was Bootsy's first proper bass. The slim neck profile, coupled with the direct, punchy tone, make a Fender Jazz perfect for Funk bass players.

Ampeg made the main bass amps of the time and Bootsy tended to use the SVT head live. You will see his image next to a whole range of modern pedals these days, but back in the day he was recognised as one of the first bass players to embrace effects. One of his most used was the Musictronics Mu-Tron III Envelope Filter. Electro Harmonix do something similar called the Q Tron and it's a fraction of the price. An envelope filter is a must for the Funk bass player, but make sure you use it sparingly.

Graham is most famous for his white Moon bass. Moon are a Japanese company and Graham has played them for decades. Again, it is influenced by the Fender Jazz with two single coil pickups and a comfortable neck profile. Search on YouTube for "Larry Graham phaser" and you will hear one of the most amazing sounds to emanate from the bass guitar! Sadly, the Roland Jet Phaser has been discontinued.

Sound processing innovations accelerated right around the time Funk emerged and both players were quick to latch on to them.

Recommended Listening

Cold Sweat – James Brown

Super Bad – James Brown

Breakdown – Parliament

If You Want Me to Stay – Sly & The Family Stone

Thank You (Falettinme Be Mice Elf Agin) – Sly & The Family Stone

Hair – Graham Central Station

Bootsy Collins

Our first example pays homage to the very first Funk song, *Cold Sweat*. Much Funk used vocabulary from RnB and Soul, and dominant 7 chords were very popular.

Example 1a outlines the notes of the G7 chord (G, B, D, F) with passing notes targeting the final D.

G7 arpeggio

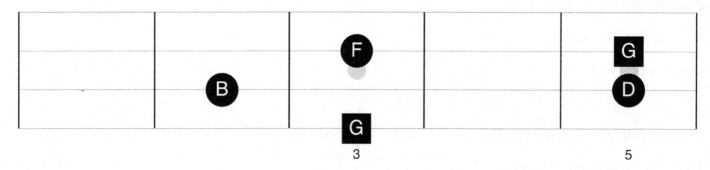

In this groove, you'll hear two common Funk devices: syncopation and repetition. Lock onto the drum beat and play as tightly as you can, but take care not to rush any of the notes that follow an 1/8th note rest.

Remember to download all the audio examples, drum loops and backing tracks at **www.fundamental-changes. com**. Many of the grooves in this book have full backing tracks and this is one of them.

Example 1a

The next groove is based around the same arpeggio and adds a classic blues movement from the minor 3rd to the major 3rd of the scale. To play this one right, you'll need to rake the final three notes of bar one with one finger.

This example can be broken down into the fretboard pattern below and is easy to use in your own playing. Try moving from the root to the b3 and then landing on the major 3 before adding in other notes from the arpeggio above.

Minor/Major 3rd pattern

Example 1b

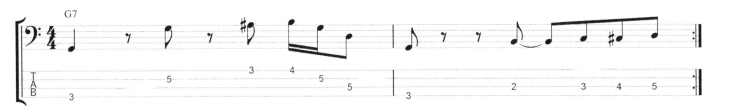

The root, 5th, b7, and octave intervals play a huge role in Funk basslines so make sure you know their locations by studying the diagram below before working through this example. Example 1c contains just these four notes which are all essential ingredients in our Funk stew!

Root/5th/m7/octave: the funk formula

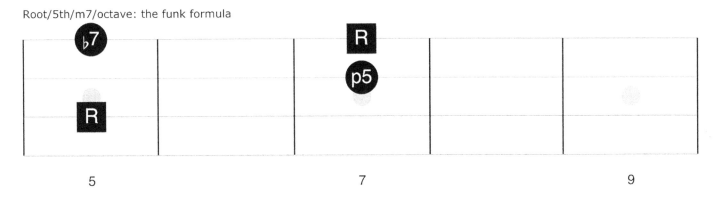

Ensure you rake from the C on the 5th fret to the A on the 7th as it'll keep the groove tight and smooth, but concentrate on keeping each note short and punchy. The lengths of the notes you play are very important, so pay close attention to the *ends* of your notes to make sure they finish in the right place. As with every example in this book, always tap your foot to make the beat a physical part of your body.

Example 1c

The next line is a common ii V chord progression in the key of B Major (C#m, F#7). Focus on the transition from the C# on the 6th fret to the B on the 2nd fret as it might catch you out at first. You'll need to shift your hand quickly and confidently to move position and stay in time.

Example 1d

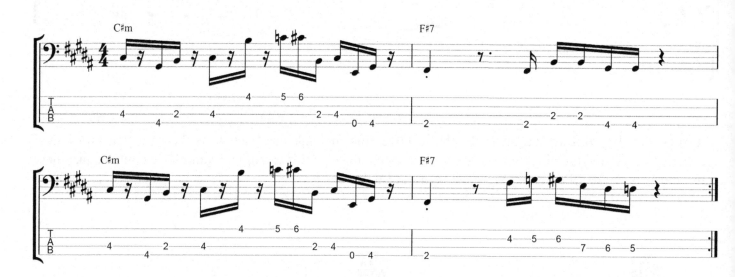

Short notes leave more room for space and those gaps contribute so much to the groove. Often what you don't play is as important as what you do.

Funk players often use rests to execute quick hand shifts and doing so makes intricate lines far less daunting! Notice how the first few notes are played higher up on the D string. This is another tactic to avoid a big shift since the notes an octave apart are played on the same string.

Example 1e

Larry Graham

With the exception of the first note, every note in Example 1f is played on *off beats*. These can be tricky to place so make sure your foot is tapping on the beat to create a strong reference point.

Playing the A on the 5th fret will give you far more control than plucking the open string. Just release the pressure slightly with your fretting hand finger to stop the note.

Since the groove played is over an Am7 chord you can use the Funk formula pattern (root, 5th, b7, octave) to create your own fills. Import the drum loop into your software then first practise nailing the syncopated line before adding your own touch with some extra notes chosen from the diagram below.

Root/5th/m7/octave of Am

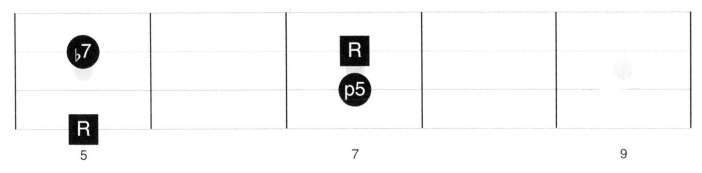

Example 1f

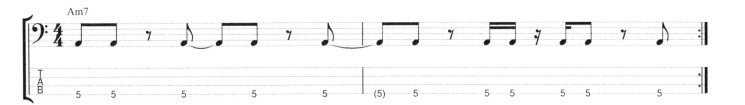

While minor chords are more common in Funk, major chords also feature regularly.

This next line is a I V chord progression in the key of F Major (F, C). Use the suggested fingering in bar two to slide into the notes on the 5th fret from fret 3. This is a very useful way to efficiently slide to different notes in a single position on the neck.

Example 1g

A *hammer-on from nowhere* is when you produce a note by hammering down on it with a fretting hand finger. Slap the open E then hammer onto the 3rd fret with your second finger.

Isolate the slides in bar one and work on the interplay between both hands, making sure not to rush each slide.

Examples 1h, i and j are all in the same key so try joining them up. This one has a backing track.

Example 1h

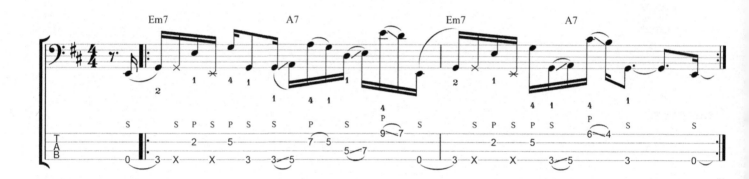

Example 1i introduces another classic Funk bass technique, the *shake* (shown by the squiggle over the last note). Quickly slide your first finger back and forth between frets 5 and 6.

When using shakes in your own lines, use a bit of discretion! It's like using too much salt – just enough enhances things but too much ruins it.

Example 1i

Funk rhythms borrow heavily from African music traditions. Example 1j is a repetitive figure that uses the bass like a drum.

First get this to groove without a metronome, then use the drum backing loop. If you can get heads bobbing when playing on your own, you know your time/feel is good.

Slapping and popping on the same string is difficult, so focus especially on the G on fret 5. Angle your slapping hand slightly so that both your thumb and first finger can access the D string comfortably.

Example 1j

Chapter Two – '70s Disco

The players: Bernard Edwards, Mark Adams, Verdine White

If the '80s heralded the big-haired guitar hero, the music of the '70s belonged to Disco and the bass player. Disco songs were characterised by pulsating basslines and four-to-the-floor drumbeats.

Songs like *Everybody Dance* and *Slide* contain some of mainstream music's funkiest moments, and this chapter focuses on disco along with the funky chart music of the 1970s.

Disco encapsulates a few musical styles, including early Funk, Pop, and Soul. Its purpose was simple: to get clubbers on the dancefloor, and the rhythm section was the driving force. Disco went out of fashion towards the end of the '70s and early '80s, but the best songs are timeless and their basslines are a rich vein for Funk aficionados.

One of the most influential bass players of this era was Bernard Edwards. Most famous for playing in Chic alongside Nile Rodgers, he was also a prolific producer. Artists he produced or played for include Sister Sledge, Diana Ross, Robert Palmer and Duran Duran.

His flowing riff-based lines and impeccable feel can be heard on many hits that still get airplay today. While Edwards mainly played fingerstyle, he sometimes used his fingers as a plectrum to get a focussed, urgent tone. That magical technique is explored later.

Mark Adams is one of the least-known players in this book and was in one of the most underrated bands, Slave. While they didn't achieve anywhere near the success of bands like Chic, they left a legacy every Funk fan should check out.

Adams' huge tone, use of legato, slides, shakes, and all manner of articulations influenced hordes of bass players. In fact, listen to his playing on *Slide* from the eponymous 1977 *Slave* album and you can hear (perhaps) where Neil Jason got the idea for his slides in *Some Skunk Funk*.

Terrifyingly, he was only sixteen years old when he recorded *Slide*. His playing is raw but belies his youth. By the time Stone Jam came along in 1980 he had found his voice, using slap, fingerstyle and his trademark slides to stamp his mark on Slave's disco-funk. Adams was a groove monster.

Earth Wind & Fire were a hit-making force that spanned many genres and Verdine White must have clocked the most distance ever travelled on stage with his entertaining dance moves. They sold over ninety million records, won six Grammys and White's lines always managed to remain melodic, groovy and prominent.

Gear checklist: Bernard Edwards had a distinctive punchy sound, produced through a combination of his active MusicMan StingRay bass and his incredibly precise plucking hand technique. The StingRay was one of the first active, mass market production basses (one of Leo Fender's innovations after selling Fender to CBS).

The active circuit allowed the player to boost frequencies using controls on the instrument. The sound was more aggressive than a passive bass and was a huge part of Edwards' sound.

The StingRay, with its single humbucker, remains a standard for Funk bass instruments. Other configurations have been produced since the sale of MusicMan to Ernie Ball, but for an authentic Funk sound and solid investment, a pre-Ernie Ball StingRay is a good bet.

Mark Adams played Fender Jazz basses and Alembics. His main bass was a Fender Jazz, modded with three pickups – the third placed near the neck. He used chorus and flanger pedals as part of his sound too, which you can hear on *Sizzlin' Hot*.

A big part of the appeal of Funk bass is that the bass is so upfront in the mix. For those people who don't really know what the bass does, play them a Slave tune and they'll soon get it!

Verdine White's first instrument was a Fender Telecaster bass. He then went on to use Fender Jazz and Precision basses, a Yamaha BB-3000, and currently plays a Sadowsky signature model featuring P-J pickups. He doesn't tend to use effects and records straight to the desk, sometimes micing up an Ampeg B15.

Recommended Listening

Everybody Dance – Chic

Good Times – Chic

Le Freak – Chic

Slide – Slave

Stone Jam – Slave

Just a Touch of Love – Slave

Boogie Wonderland – Earth Wind & Fire

In the Stone – Earth Wind & Fire

Can't Let Go – Earth Wind & Fire

Bernard Edwards

In our first Bernard Edwards-style line, the notes after the dotted 1/8th note rests fall on the fourth 1/16th note of the beat. To play these precisely, subdivide the beat by counting "1-e-&-a" and place the note on the "a". This is a great way to align yourself to tricky 1/16th note rhythms.

Example 2a

To create memorable hooks, Edwards often used similar rhythms and patterns on each chord. The next groove uses the root, octave, b7, and 5th, so use the same fingering pattern throughout. Target the ghost notes at the end of each riff to shift your hand quickly to the next position.

Example 2b

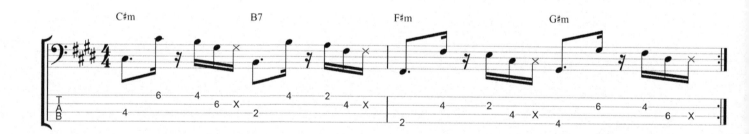

The next two examples use Edwards' pioneering technique called *chucking* (listen to the intro of *Everybody Dance* by Chic). To do this, hold your thumb and index finger together as if you were holding a plectrum and use the fingernail of your index finger for downstrokes and the fleshy tip for upstrokes.

Keep your picking hand constantly moving in a steady stream of 1/16th notes. This is absolutely the key to getting this technique to work. To make the notes pop a little more, add a touch of palm muting.

Make sure your fretting hand fingers stay close to the fretboard at all times.

Check out the accompanying video for a full tutorial on this cool technique:

https://geni.us/funkvideos

Example 2c

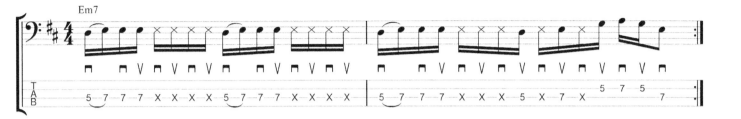

The next line uses the same lick at the start then moves up an octave. After the first four notes, play the ghost notes on the open D string as you shift your fretting hand to the D on the 7th fret.

Maintain the constant motion in the picking hand and the easy, clean shifting in the fretting hand.

Example 2d

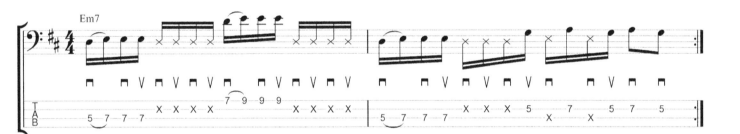

The *Good Times* bassline also inspired another monster in *Another One Bites the Dust*. Example 2e uses the same chord progression: a ii V in the key of D Major (Em7 to A7).

Keep the hammer-ons in bar four nice and controlled and make sure the note you hammer onto is the same volume as the plucked one.

Example 2e

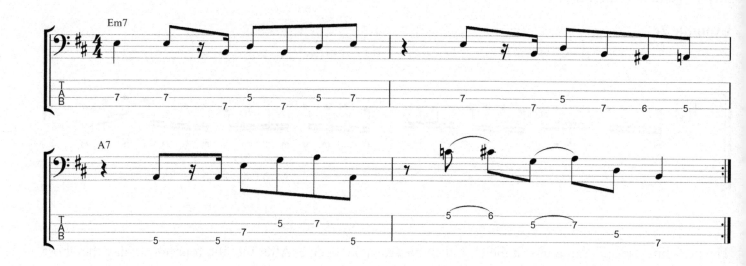

The Minor Blues and Dorian scales are often used in Funk bass. Let's take a closer look at them.

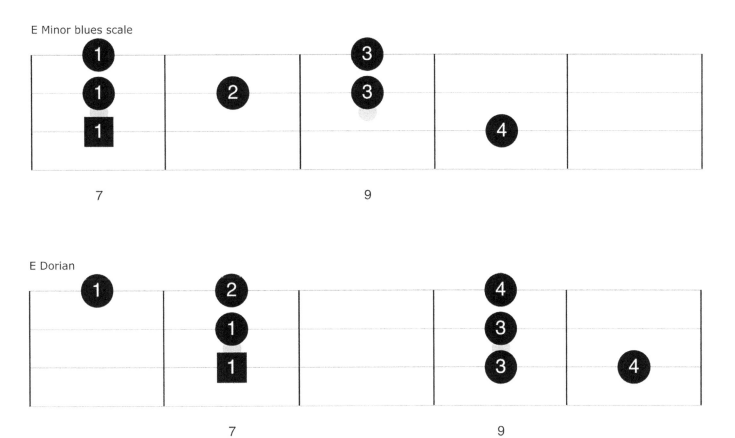

Memorise these scales as you will use them a lot. Use the diagrams to improvise your own fills over Example 2f. Fills are often played at the end of phrases, so go for it in bar four.

Mute the open E by anchoring your plucking hand thumb on the E string after you've plucked it in the final bar to stop it running into the following notes.

Example 2f

The next groove begins with a bass fill before launching into a muscular repeated hook. Work hard on bar one as the hammer-on followed by a ghost note can be quite hard to time well.

The main groove is fairly simple but focus on playing it with attitude and aggression.

Example 2g

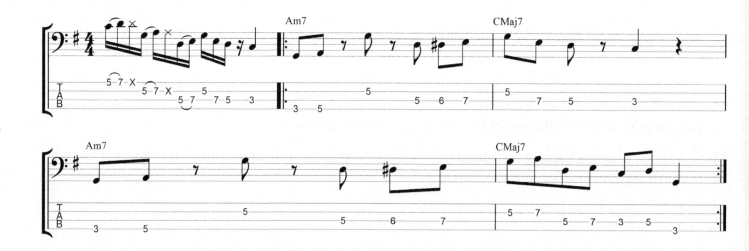

In Example 2h, look at the G on the 3rd fret while you're executing the shake on the 14th so you can get there accurately without missing a beat.

To play the slide on the last note, slide in from one of the lower frets (around fret 3) and then back using one pluck only. Practice altering the speed of the slide as well as the attack of the plucked note. There are many ways you can play slides, so put your own stamp on it. Listen to the audio to hear how I do it.

Example 2h

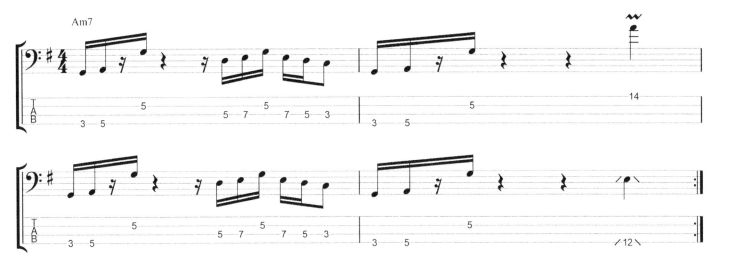

Focus on the first eight notes of this next line and play them slowly while you get the slap/pop pattern down. Use your third or fourth finger for the notes on the 5th fret.

Set your metronome to a slow tempo (say 50 BPM) and feel the clicks on beats two and four. This simulates the back beat and will help your timing. Try this at a few different tempos then use the backing track.

Example 2i

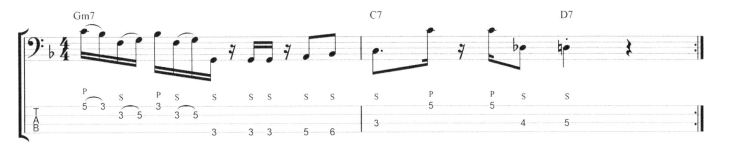

Examples 2j and 2i can be played together as they both use G Dorian.

After plucking the first note, play the F on the 3rd fret with the same fingertip. Alternatively, you can use a lower part of your first finger, barring slightly to catch the F. Slide to the 12th fret with your third finger, then play the shake with your first finger.

Example 2j

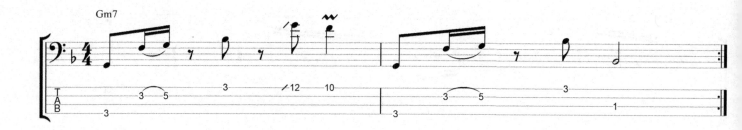

Verdine White

The first Verdine White-style bassline has a 1/16th note swing that creates a bouncy groove.

Example 2k

Example 2l uses octaves to outline a V I IV chord progression in the key of G Major. At the end of bar one you might find it easier to barre the notes on the 5th fret. Play the D with your fingertip, then use the lower part of the same finger to fret the C.

The run at the end of the last bar requires a very quick hand shift, so be prepared.

Example 2l

Example 2m uses a similar approach to *In the Stone* by Earth Wind and Fire, which is a beautiful example of interesting chords in a Pop/Funk song. It's syncopated, melodic, and lets the space do the talking.

We use strategic pops in gaps between the main line to create a dragging, yet energetic groove. The dotted 1/8th note rests either side of the pops give you just enough time to get there and back to the fretted notes. Still, you will need to transition from plucking to slapping quickly, so focus on that hand.

Example 2m

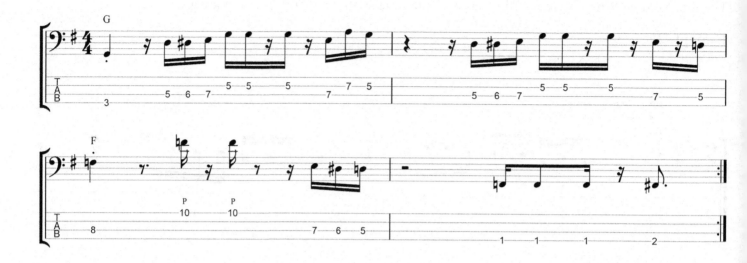

Example 2n approaches each root note chromatically from either above or below. This is a really effective device to use when transitioning between chords.

It can be easy to rush the 1/16th notes after the rests on beats two and four, so pay particular attention to those points. There's a backing track for this example so go and have some fun with it.

Example 2n

In this final example, follow the suggested fretting hand fingering closely. You will notice a few subtle but quick hand shifts that need to be played very precisely. Practise this along with the backing track.

Example 2o

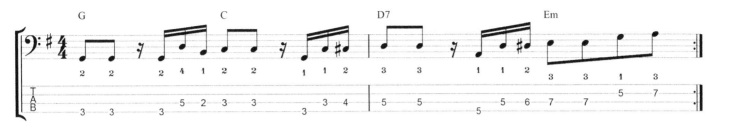

Chapter Three – 1/16th Note Funk

The players: Francis "Rocco" Prestia, Jaco Pastorius, Bobby Vega

Francis "Rocco" Prestia's influences came from the James Brown and Motown stables, but he himself wrote the book on 1/16th note basslines. Both Jaco Pastorius and Bobby Vega cite Rocco as a huge influence.

The early 1970s saw Rocco's band, Tower of Power, move more towards Funk and it was around this time that he started punctuating his basslines with machine-gun-like 1/16th notes. This required immense technique and stamina and turned the bass into a secondary percussion instrument.

The constant stream of notes, often accompanied by left hand muting and ghost notes, added an intense, insistent groove to the music. One of Tower of Power's main features is the incredibly tight horn section, and Rocco and his drumming sidekick David Garibaldi would be called on to catch horn stabs in the middle of a groove.

Jaco Pastorius, alongside James Jamerson, is perhaps *the* most influential bass player of all time, but even he had to get some of his ideas from other sources. *Come On, Come Over* from his 1976 solo album is a huge nod to Rocco's style. His punchy fretless bass sound, ferocious technique, and impeccable timing lent itself well to Funk. Jaco often fell back on crafted lines to fit over certain chords and many of his most memorable phrases featured cascades of 1/16ths.

Rocco and Jaco's spirit can be heard all over the music of modern bass heroes such as Joe Dart of Vulfpeck. Listen to *Dean Town* for a great example.

Bobby Vega is a guy with every trick in the box as well as the musicality to back it up. He's a true master of the instrument, perhaps best known for his plectrum work. The section of the chapter dedicated to him will focus solely on the pick.

Yet another teenage prodigy, he recorded *I Get High On You* by Sly Stone in 1973 at the age of 16. When Rocco had health problems, it was Bobby Vega who got the call to step in. That raised his profile a little, but he's still relatively unknown. His stock is rising rapidly though, mainly due to his stellar appearances on various YouTube videos. Slap, taps, ghost notes, raking, sweep picking, artificial harmonics, fingerstyle, and picking all play a part of his sound. He is a true Funk virtuoso.

Gear Checklist: Rocco's sound is round, warm and old school. He used to play Fender Precision basses and his technique is based around alternate plucking with the index and middle fingers. Lately, he endorses ESP basses with a PJ pickup configuration. His sound has changed over the years, but his tone very much comes from his hands. Left hand muting is one unusual technique he uses to simulate the sound of a bass with foam mute. The muting almost acts like a compressor, making the notes pop out in the mix. He never uses effects.

Jaco's "Bass of Doom" was his de-fretted 1962 Fender Jazz bass. The neck width at the nut was narrower than other basses making it slightly easier to get around. Jaco's double-jointed large hands coupled with the bass allowed him to fly around the neck. To get the Jaco tone, solo your back pickup (if you have one) and play closer to the bridge for a tighter more percussive sound.

Bobby Vega tends to favour vintage Fender Jazz and Precision basses. He sounds like himself on whatever instrument he plays. He can coax a huge variety of tones out of different basses with flat wound or stainless-steel strings. Vega gives us a timely reminder not to get too bogged down by gear. He uses yellow Dunlop .73mm plectrums.

Recommended Listening

Only So Much Oil in The Ground – Tower Of Power

What Is Hip? - Tower Of Power

Soul With a Capital "S" - Tower Of Power

Ain't Nothing But a Party – Brian Melvin's Night Food

Come On Come Over – Jaco Pastorius

The Chicken – Jaco Pastorius

I Get High on You – Sly Stone

Buttermilk – Sketches of Bob

Search "Bobby Vega" on YouTube for loads of amazing clips

Francis "Rocco" Prestia

The notes in Example 3a closely outline a D7 chord (D, F#, A, C) and it's essential to play each note fretted to make the line easier to play consistently. Make sure both hands are relaxed and ready to shift to a higher string, or across the neck.

The next five examples can be practised together as they use similar harmonies.

Example 3a

The next example has a backing track. Play the first bar in third position using your first finger for the G on the 3rd fret. In bar two shift into fifth *position* by playing the fret 5 note with your first finger. (A position on the bass is dictated by which fret your first finger is on when you line up one finger per fret).

Example 3b

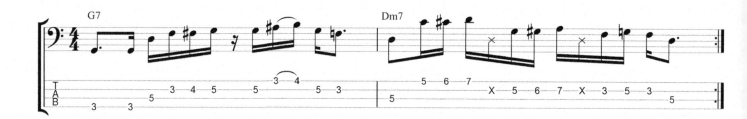

Left hand muting is a trademark Rocco technique, which turns the fretting hand into a mute. To do it you'll normally fret any notes with your first and second fingers, leaving the third and fourth fingers to gently touch the strings – not to completely choke the note, but enough to lightly dampen it.

Combined with ghosting, the notes become shorter and more percussive. Your fretting hand will have to move way more than you're used to, so be prepared to shift across the neck.

Example 3c

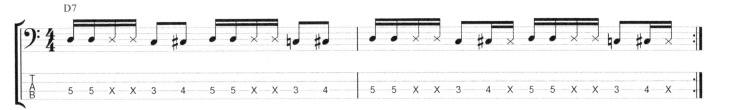

Many bass players overlook the importance of learning to play simple 1/16th note lines consistently, without any changes in volume or speed. The next groove will help you practice this and also test your stamina and endurance. To move to the next level, go and learn *What Is Hip?* – a thorn in the side of many bass players!

If the drum backing track is a little quick on this one, set your metronome to a slower tempo and build up from there.

Example 3d

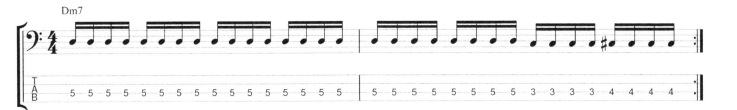

The next groove includes fifths on adjacent strings, an idea found on another Tower of Power classic *Funk the Dumb Stuff*.

This line calls for you to go from the 3rd to the 12th frets in no time at all, so make sure your fretting hand glides across the neck smoothly and swiftly. Using the same fingers to fret the notes each time you slide will avoid you having to change fingering pattern.

Example 3e

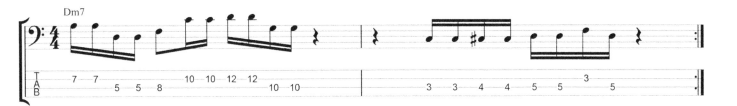

Jaco Pastorius

Jaco loved to use soul and funk-inspired licks, coming up with a number of stock lines that he used throughout his career. Example 3f is a 1/16th note line you can use over minor chords (Am in this case).

Break this line down into two beat chunks as there's a fair bit going on. Where you see the ghost notes, rake your index finger to the G on the 3rd fret to allow the line to flow better than if you plucked all the notes. Follow the suggested fingering pattern but do feel free to use your fourth finger instead of the third finger.

Example 3f

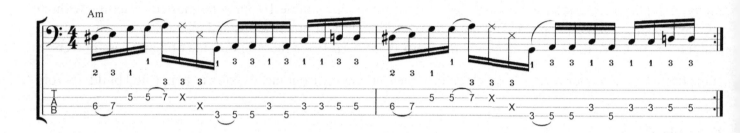

Similar ideas are used over a C7 chord for this next groove. Once more, take this beat by beat. The pull-off and hammer-on (beats three and four) really make this phrase sing. Don't rush them and aim to keep those articulations an equal volume to the plucked notes.

Play examples 3f and 3g together as the chords work well together.

Example 3g

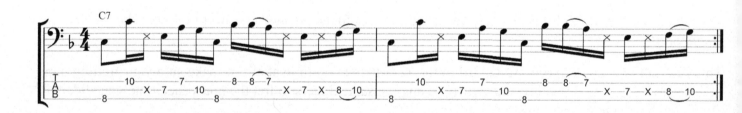

In the next example, I find it easier to rake the notes on adjacent strings on beat three, bar one. Control the fretting hand fingers and time their release so each note sounds without ringing into the next.

Once you've plucked the first double-stop, let your fretting hand do all the rhythmic work with the slides.

Example 3h

If you play the root note of a major chord on the A string, you get instant access to the 5th and 6th intervals (the B on the 9th fret and the C# on the 6th fret). This little root, 5, 6 pattern is something Jaco used a lot. It's a handy idea you can use in many styles of music.

Play the final note of bar three with your second finger then quickly transition so that your fourth finger jumps to the same note. This gets you into position for the notes in the final bar. That move is essential to play this line smoothly and accurately.

Example 3i

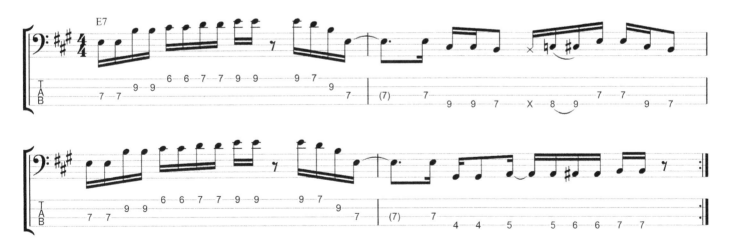

In the next line, use your third finger instead of your fourth in bars one and two if it's easier but, otherwise, follow the fingering suggestions. The patterns in bars three and four are exactly the same, so just make sure to shift quickly from one root note to the next (D on the 5th fret to C on the 3rd).

Example 3j

Bobby Vega

The next five examples focus on Bobby Vega's extraordinary plectrum technique. Central to his style is his use of constant pick motion. Check the video out for a detailed explanation: **https://geni.us/funkvideos**

Keep your picking hand going in a continuous down-up movement, even when you're not playing a note, as this will keep you locked to the rhythmic "grid". Study the pick markings and you'll see this constant motion. The first symbol ⊓ is a down stroke and (weirdly) the one that looks like a "v" ∨ is the up stroke. Beats two and four are accented to simulate the feel of a drummer's snare, which is a stock Vega trick, and adds an inordinate amount of groove to proceedings.

If it's your first time with a plectrum, this line might feel awkward, but with regular practice you'll get it together no problem.

Example 3k

There's some string skipping in the next example, so keep your picking hand wrist loose to let it move quickly when crossing strings.

The staccato notes are the key to making this line feel great, so listen to the audio example carefully. Notice how the 1/8th notes at the end of each bar fall naturally under a down stroke.

Example 3l

Example 3m uses the notes of the E Mixolydian mode over an E7 chord. Accent every beat to create an insistent heavy groove. You'll need to be very quick when you slide to the A on the 12th fret and when sliding back downwards from fret 11.

As a self-learning exercise, use the diagram below to help you write similar lines across the A string. Restricting yourself in this way is a great creative process that can lead to some fresh ideas. Note that the root note is the square E. Play an open string E as you play through this shape. This will really get your ears around this mode.

E Mixolydian on the A string

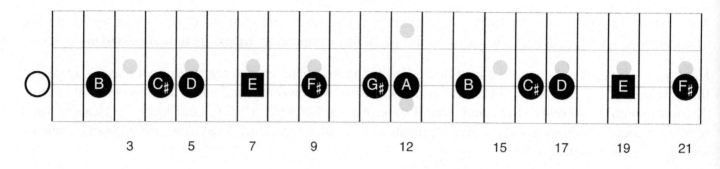

Example 3m

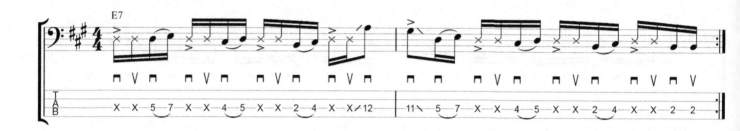

Now it's time for a string skipping extravaganza using octave jumps.

When recording or playing in a band, it's not always desirable to play all the ghost notes in the previous examples. Cutting off the note right before the rest lets the snare drum land on its own on beats two and four. This is a great way to sound really tight with the drummer.

There's a backing track to play along to for this one, so be sure to download it and jam along once you're up to speed.

Example 3n

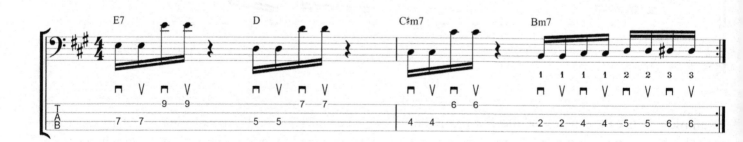

The *fretting hand pat* technique is how you'll produce the ghost notes after the hammer-ons in the next line.

Isolate the notes in beat one first before working on the rest of the line, as they're likely to cause you the most problems.

Pay attention to the sliding double-stops at the end. The rests give you time to get in position.

Example 3o

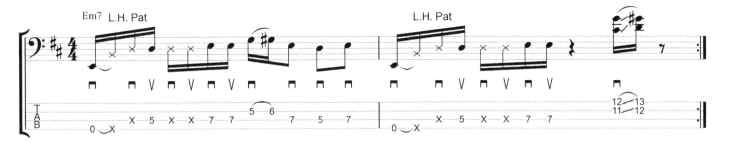

Chapter Four – Jazz Funk

The players: Paul Jackson, Abraham Laboriel, Incognito

The melting pot of Jazz Funk contains Bossa Nova, Blues, Bebop, African rhythms, Ragtime, RnB and Gospel. The jazz-funk pioneers of the 1970s focused heavily on the Funk, with artists like Miles Davis and Herbie Hancock veering towards electric instruments and strong backbeats.

Many of the genre's finest moments were instrumentals which gave the musicians more scope to shine than in the vocal-led Funk that preceded.

Perhaps the most famous album of the genre is Herbie Hancock's 1973 *Head Hunters* album featuring Paul Jackson on bass. There are four tracks on the album and the first, *Chameleon*, is 15:41 long as the music was designed less for the dance floor and more for the art itself. Jackson played repeating grooves, anchoring the ship, so the other musicians could go off and explore, while Hancock wrote unison lines for the whole band to play – something not so common in more traditional Funk styles.

Jackson mainly used fingerstyle technique and had a wonderful round, full sound that sat well in any mix.

Born in Mexico City in 1947, Abe Laboriel is one of the most recorded session bass players of all time and also one of the most unique technicians. He often added techniques he was hearing from his classical guitar training that resulted in shocking levels of technical proficiency, coupled with a huge tone and groove.

His tone is unique due to the way he plucks and attacks the strings. He often uses his nails, so that it sounds like he's playing with a plectrum. Rasgueados, classical fingerstyle techniques, slap and fast alternate plucking make up an exciting playbook.

Laboriel features in this chapter due to his sheer level of recorded output. You'll have heard him on tracks such as Dolly Parton's *9 to 5*, right through to *Let It Go* from Frozen, but he was the go-to guy for many Jazz Funk artists (including Quincy Jones, Lee Ritenour and Al Jarreau).

With their first album, *Jazz Funk*, Incognito have to be included to complete this chapter. A whole host of UK bass legends have passed through this Funk-jazz school including Julian Crampton, Randy Hope-Taylor and Francis Hylton. What unites them in the context of Incognito is impeccable groove and beautifully crafted lines. Bass is at the epicentre of their mostly song-based music. If you like Funk and you like great songs, you would do well to immerse yourself in the Incognito back catalogue.

Gear Checklist: Paul Jackson's bass tone is pretty old school and evolved from the James Jamerson Fender Precision sound. It sits well in the mix and goes to show that you don't have to play Funk on a Music Man or Fender Jazz. He played a Precision on *Head Hunters*. Live he has used a Precision along with other makes, but often still with a P bass pickup.

Abe Laboriel uses five-string basses a lot, using lots of different makes but favouring Yamaha. His tone comes from his hands and the various techniques he employs. He sometimes uses notes below E when he records and, applied tastefully, their effect adds a lot to the song.

The Incognito bass players all lean towards the tried and tested Fender Jazz sound. Julian Crampton has a 75 Made in Japan reissue; Francis Hylton uses Atelier Z basses; and Randy Hope-Taylor uses Yamaha basses with two single coil pickups. All these basses are incredibly comfortable to play which really is essential when playing intricate Funk grooves.

Recommended Listening

Chameleon – Herbie Hancock

Watermelon Man – Herbie Hancock

Sly – Herbie Hancock

Fly by Night – Lee Ritenour

Rise – Herb Alpert

On Eagle's Wings – Abe Laboriel & Friends

Just Say Nothing – Incognito

Everyday – Incognito

Colibri – Incognito

Paul Jackson

Example 4a uses a trademark Jackson solid groove coupled with melodic, upper-register fills. To emulate his hypnotic style of playing play this groove on repeat for as long as you can without altering a note.

This is also a good example of where playing an open string instead of the 5th fret works incredibly well. Just make sure you control the note length with your fretting hand.

Example 4a

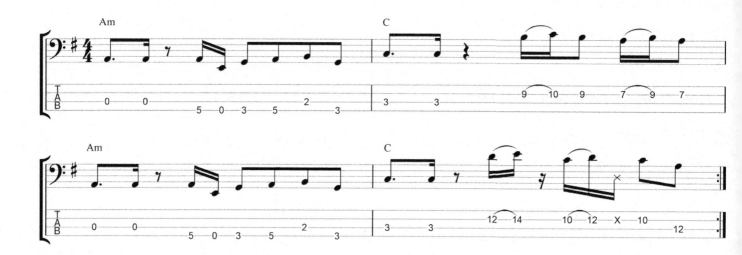

In Watermelon Man, Jackson used major tenths to great effect. They sound lovely on bass and perhaps the most famous example is the line Herbie Flowers played on *Walk on the Wild Side*.

You have two options of how to play the first two notes. Either pluck them as normal with your index and middle fingers or just use your thumb. The second option puts you in perfect position to pluck the double-stops (with your thumb and index). Try both ways.

Example 4b

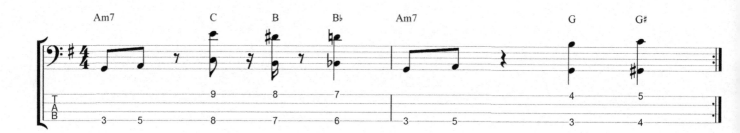

Many Herbie Hancock Jazz Funk tunes featured long hypnotic sections that could be soloed over. Here's your opportunity to improvise a little. Study the two diagrams below and use the patterns to stretch out and spice things up a little.

A Dorian

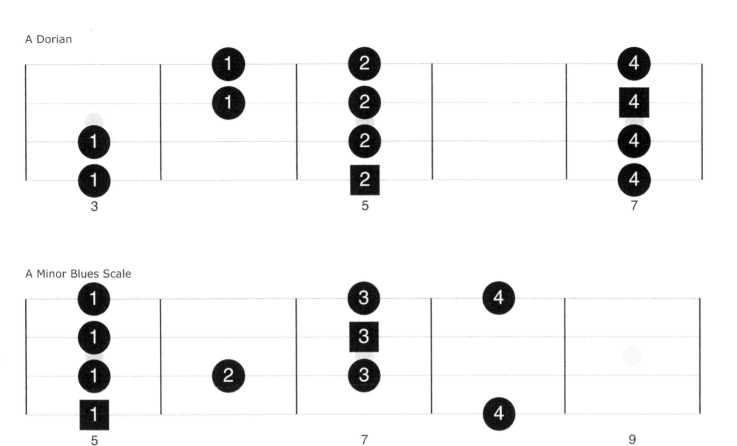

A Minor Blues Scale

These two scales are a match made in heaven. Memorise them and use them in your basslines, solos and fills (they work over minor chords).

Example 4c

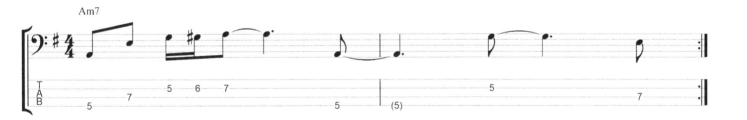

The next groove is heavily syncopated, fast and frenetic. It's best to keep a line like this in one position so that you don't need to shift your hand.

A word about tapping your foot when counting 1/16ths…

Count the 1/16th notes out loud "1e&a 2e&a 3e&a 4e&a" and learn to feel where all the 1/16ths sit in relation to your tapping foot.

When you tap your foot, it always hits the floor on a beat (1 2 3 4). Then observe your foot coming right up on the "&" before going down for the next beat.

Feeling the first 1/16th note is easy as it lands when your foot hits the floor. The "&" is also relatively easy as it's a simple offbeat 1/8th note. It's the "e" and the "a" that can be tricky to catch.

The "e" is immediately after your foot taps, but *before* it reaches the up position. The "a" is between the up position of your foot and the next tap on the floor.

Eventually, this will be internalised and will turn you into a groove guru!

Example 4d

The intro to *Chameleon* is one of the most famous basslines in Funk but it's not actually played on bass – it's Herbie's left hand, probably playing a Moog synth.

Example 4e is a nod to that great line. It's a ii V chord progression in the key of F Minor (Gm7, C7) that highlights the Dorian mode. Compare the shape for the Dorian mode to the pattern in Example 4c. Memorising both shapes will increase your options.

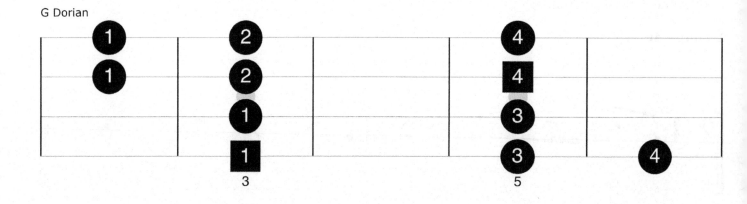

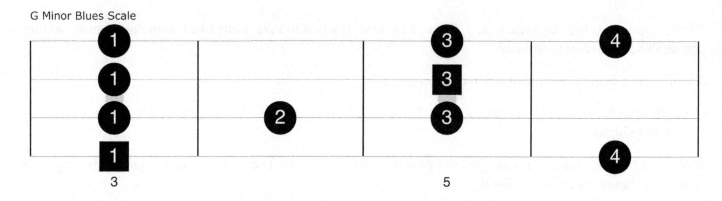

You can use the above diagrams to write some fills once you have this line under your fingers.

Example 4e

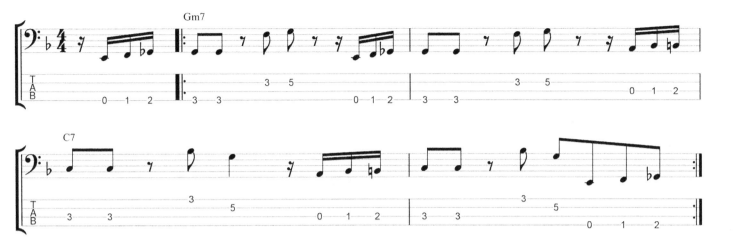

Abe Laboriel

A common element in Jazz Funk is the use of more interesting chord progressions. Example 4f contains an Fmaj7 chord which is outside of the key of G Major. You can use the F Lydian mode to play on this chord. Experiment with the notes in the following diagram over the included backing track to create your own grooves.

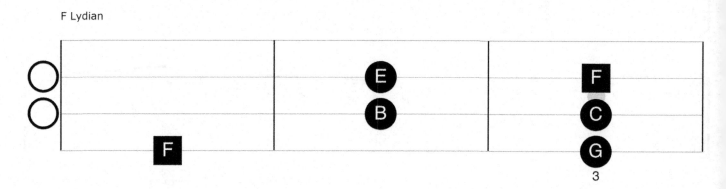

One thing to watch out for in this example is the jump back to the 3rd fret C note at the end of bar two.

Example 4f

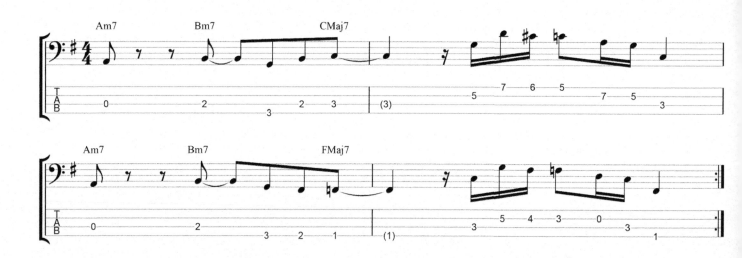

Here's another line that funks up a common jazz chord progression. Example 4g is a I vi ii V chord progression in the key of A Major (Amaj7, F#m7, Bm7, E7).

Pluck the very first note then slide into the next one on the 9th fret from below.

Example 4g

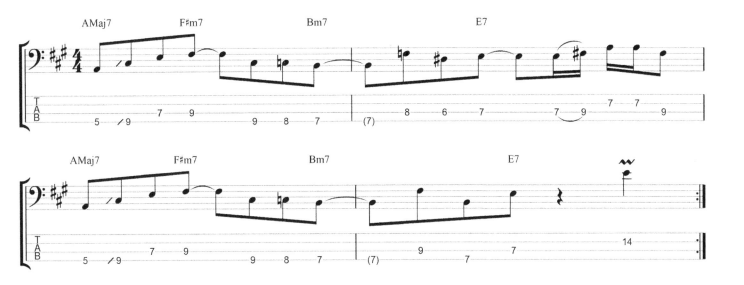

The fill in bar four of the next line infuses the Dorian mode with a chromatic note to give a strong jazzy flavour.

Loop the drum backing track and repeat this groove trying to alter the final fill each time round.

Here we can use the A Dorian mode around the 12th fret. The diagram below shows the chord, scale and chromatic tones.

Use the chromatic tones as passing notes. If you land on "safe" chord tones and use the scale tones for melody, you can't go too far wrong! There are literally hundreds of phrases to be made from the complicated looking diagram below so take your time exploring. Remember that chromatics will give you a jazzy sound so use judiciously!

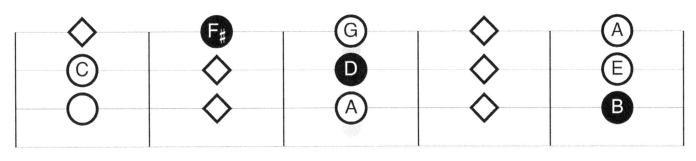

12

Hollow circles: chord tones

Filled circles: Added to the hollow circles, forms the whole scale

Diamonds: Chromatic notes/passing tones

Example 4h

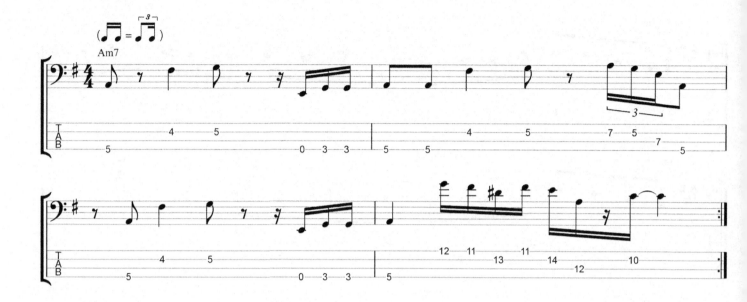

The patterns in bars one and two of this next example are identical, so take advantage of the geometric nature of the bass fretboard. You can use that pattern over any minor seventh chord.

Sliding into and out from notes is an important Funk technique, so spend time mastering the licks at the beginning of bars one and two. It can be quite tricky to get them fluent, but it's really satisfying when you do! Keep your thumb behind the neck and slide it across as you shift.

Example 4i

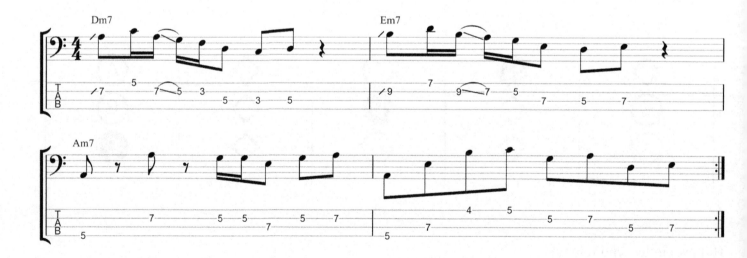

I highly recommend hunting down a copy of Abe live at the Baked Potato with Greg Mathieson, Michael Landau and Vinnie Colaiuta. It's a stunning album with loads of outrageous Jazz Funk playing. Example 4j is inspired by that kind of flair so the notation looks a little crazy. Approach this one phrase by phrase, gradually piecing the whole thing together.

Use your fretting hand to pat against the strings to create the ghost notes in the slap phrases. Then, instead of using a pick, use your plucking hand to strum where the markings are. Either use your thumb and index finger held together like a plectrum, or strum using your fingernails for the downstrokes and the fingertips for the upstrokes. For more weight you can strum using more than one finger.

Example 4j

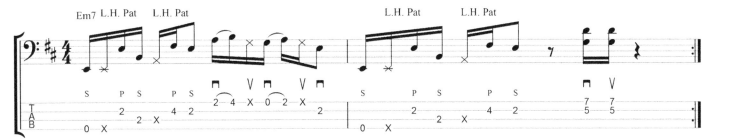

Incognito

Example 4k is a i iv III chord progression in the key of D Minor (Dm, Gm, F). Notice how notes from the chord *and* scale are used to provide melody in the line as well outline the harmony while keeping a solid groove. Try to use these elements when writing your own lines.

Example 4k

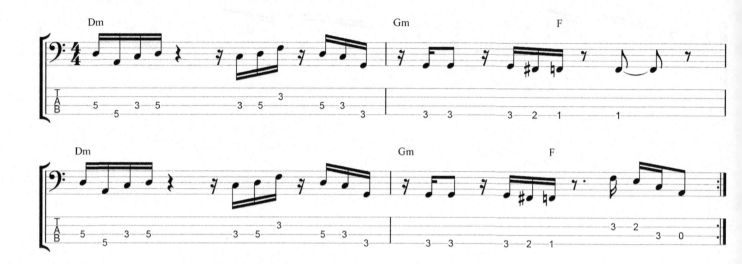

The next Funk groove uses the same chord progression but adds the ninth. This creates a cool, tuneful line and a pattern that can be used over major and minor chords. Memorise it and use it in your own playing.

Pay close attention to the fingering markings as you have to move quickly in bar two when you go from the 5th fret to the 1st fret.

Example 4l

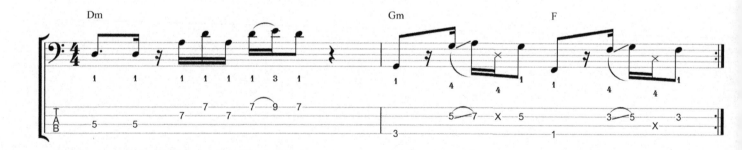

Using chromatic notes to weave a line through chord tones is a great way to add sophistication to your basslines.

To practice some beautiful sounding fills over this next line, improvise over the minor chords using each chord's minor pentatonic scale (G# Minor Pentatonic over G#m7, F# Minor Pentatonic over the F#m7).

In a band situation, keep it tasteful and don't get in the way of the groove by over-playing.

Example 4m

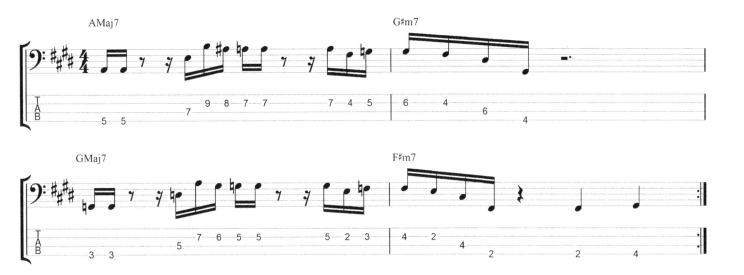

The rhythms in the next line are very syncopated but once you have the first bar down it's all the same rhythm from there. Notice how effective it can be just to play root notes with a cool rhythm.

Example 4n

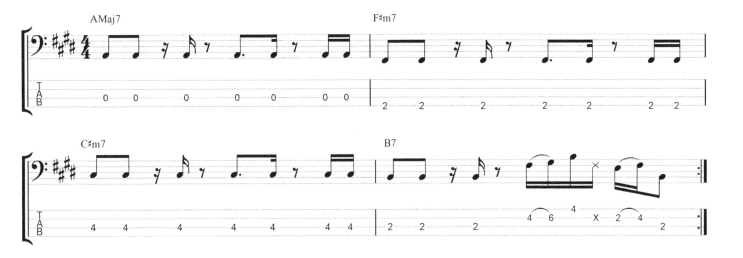

In the next groove, there's a quick shift from the 3rd to 1st fret in the first bar that takes place during the open string A. You will need to visually focus on that exact point to make the whole line flow properly. Using open strings is a good way to shift smoothly between phrases.

Example 4o

Chapter Five – Funk Rock

The players: Flea, Les Claypool, Tim Commerford

Funk and Rock are my two favourite styles of music and when I discovered *Blood Sugar Sex Magik* by Red Hot Chili Peppers I was in heaven. Since the '80s musicians like Lenny Kravitz, Living Colour and Alien Ant Farm have melded searing rock riffs with the repetitive funk rhythms to create exciting new sounds.

Funk Rock emerged in the early 1980s with bands such as Red Hot Chili Peppers, Primus and Rage Against The Machine adding elements of Metal, Hip Hop and Alternative rock into their songs.

The two styles have much in common, especially in their use of short repetitive riffs and grooves. While the songs' lyrical focus is often different, the energy and instruments are the same, and is what drew many Rock players towards Funk. In fact, many Funk Rock musicians began blending the best of the two genres together, using effects to create wild sounds.

Flea of Red Hot Chili Peppers is without doubt one of the most influential bass players of all time. He brought a high-energy stage presence to the Chilis and his basslines are built from super-fast slap and fingerstyle lines. With Chad Smith, he forms one of the greatest Funk rhythm sections of all time, and one that has created hundreds of outstanding grooves. You can clearly hear the influence of producer George Clinton on their second album *Freaky Styley*.

Les Claypool formed Primus in the early '80s and was hugely influenced by Larry Graham's slap bass style. Using all manner of taps, slaps, strums and hammer-ons, he went on to develop one of the most unique and technically advanced voices of any bass player. Listen to the theme tune for *South Park* and you'll quickly hear what Primus are all about.

Rage Against The Machine's debut album hit out against the system in 1991. It was infused with Metal, Hip Hop and Funk and remains a masterclass in riff making. Tim Commerford held the low end down, playing unison lines with the pioneering tone-master Tom Morello on guitar. Fairly traditional in his technique, Timmy C's tone is a closely guarded secret (although I'll show you how to get somewhere near it).

Gear Checklist: Flea is a multimillionaire with various bass endorsements. In his Funk Rock heyday, he played Music Man StingRay basses. Much of *Blood Sugar Sex Magik* was recorded with a Wal Mk2 bass and he often used an Electro-Harmonix Q-Tron envelope filter. That's a classic Funk bass tone with a friendly price tag. He has a signature Fender Flea bass with MM style pickups that is modelled on his shell pink '61 Jazz bass.

Claypool is best known for his Carl Thompson custom basses including his six-string fretless. He probably has the most distinctive tone of any bass player, which includes some harmonic saturation via a fairly subtle overdrive. You can get this tone by using any drive pedal with the gain raised until it replicates the sound of valves breaking up slightly.

Tim Commerford uses Fender Jazz or MusicMan StingRay basses and a fair amount of distortion but is very careful about revealing his tone secrets and uses all kinds of custom pedals to get his sound. To get close to his tone you can use a blender pedal to retain your low end while dialling in large amounts of fuzz. This is a great way to maintain your bass frequencies while getting a full and distorted sound.

Recommended Listening

Yertle The Turtle – Red Hot Chili Peppers

Freaky Styley – Red Hot Chili Peppers

Higher Ground – Red Hot Chili Peppers

Silly Putty – Primus

Tommy the Cat – Primus

Golden Boy – Primus

Guerrilla Radio – Rage Against The Machine

Wake Up – Rage Against The Machine

Know Your Enemy – Rage Against The Machine

Flea

Example 5a begins with a bouncy, melodic groove in the key of G Minor. Slide to the 12th fret with your third finger immediately after plucking the G on fret 3 (spot the *Give It Away* influence…).

When you play the 1/8th notes in bar two, keep the first slightly shorter than the second. This makes them feel very different to playing them all evenly. Listen to the audio for clarification.

Example 5a

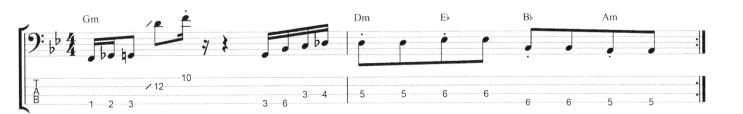

The first few Chili Peppers albums are littered with funky riffs that use very simple scales – often the minor pentatonic and blues scales. Notice how effective it can be to use simple notes played with flair and syncopation.

Keep each note short and pluck closer to the bridge to get a tight, punchy sound. Use your third and fourth fingers together to get the vibrato on the last note.

Often, the difference between a Funk and a Rock line is the attitude it's played with. Experiment on this groove by striking the strings with a heavier, more aggressive touch to create a rockier tone.

Example 5b

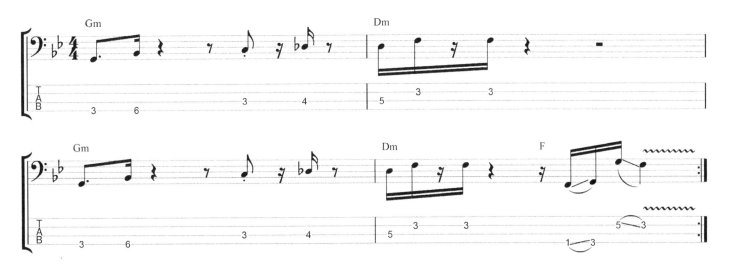

Another of Flea's favourite scales is the Dorian mode which is used all over *Blood Sugar Sex Magik*.

In this line, the b3 against the major 6th gives the Funk flavour. Try it in your own lines and use this example to create some Dorian fills using the pattern below. The root, b3, major 6th and b7 are highlighted (G, Bb, E, F) as they sound so good together.

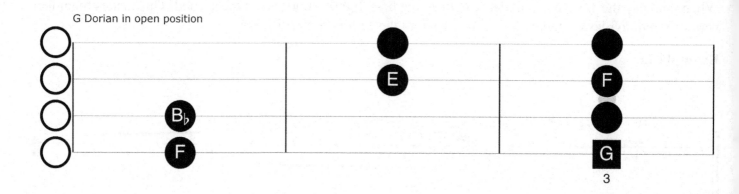

Example 5c

The 1/16th note shuffle is a favourite Funk feel and one you should definitely internalise. Cut the notes off quickly before they flatten the groove and use the hammer-on at the end of bar two to get your first finger quickly back into position ready for the repeat.

Example 5d

Slap featured heavily on many of Flea's Funk Rock basslines and Example 5e is a twist on his classic interpretation of Stevie Wonder's *Higher Ground*. This one moves around a lot, so it's important to check out the fingerings. Use the open E string to quickly shift from the slapped E on the 7th fret to the G on the 3rd fret.

Example 5e

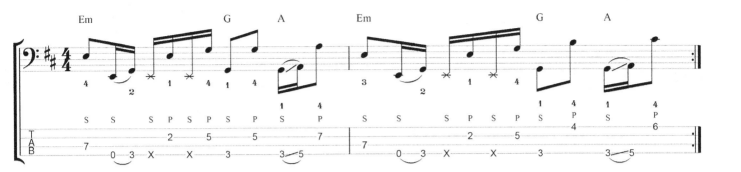

Les Claypool

Example 5f uses a Larry Graham and Stanley Clarke inspired slap technique to create a highly rhythmic groove using the E Minor Pentatonic scale. The 1/8th notes are played with a swing feel so make sure you nail that. Keep your wrist loose and just use your thumb throughout.

Example 5f

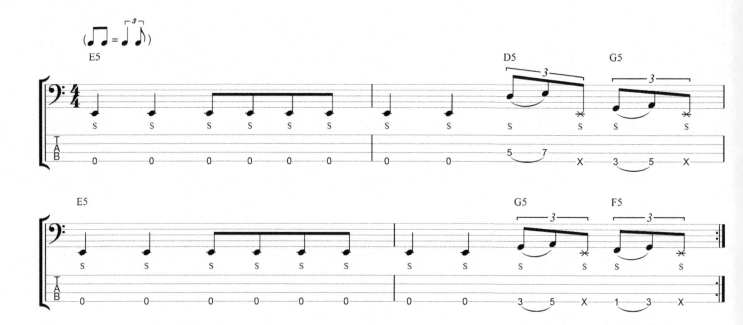

Example 5g contains *power chords* which are formed by a root and fifth played together. You'll need to transition from slap to strum and the easiest way do this is to use your fingernails to strum downwards.

The triplet rhythms here are made for slap and form the basis of many tricky-sounding phrases.

Example 5g

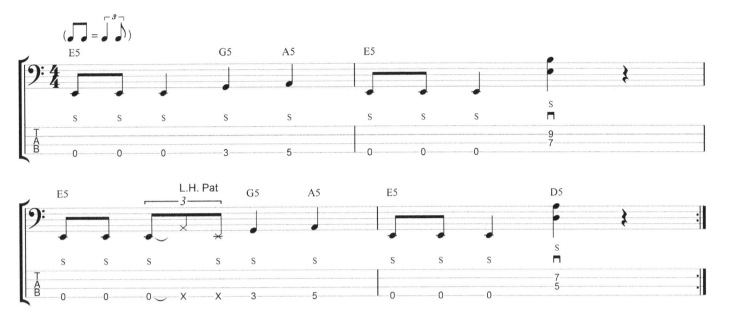

The next line is angular and doesn't stick to any real key centre.

The "T" symbol indicates a fretting hand tap. Hammer your fretting hand pinkie finger down onto the fret to create the note.

Muting is the key to making this line sounding clean. Use the tip of your fretting hand first finger to mute the underside of the E string as you play the notes on the A string. This one's quite complex so I recommend checking out the video lesson: **https://geni.us/funkvideos**

Example 5h

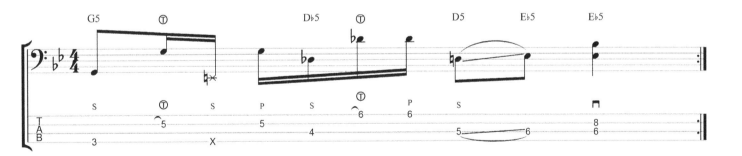

Example 5i uses some interesting articulations to create a smooth line. Pluck the 5th fret, then hammer on to 6 and 7 in one continuous movement, then use your index finger to rake across the strings.

Example 5i

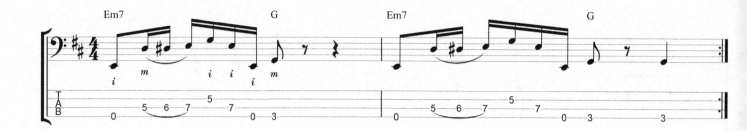

Let's add a trademark Claypool slap and strum to the previous example. Here you'll have to transition your fretting hand quickly into position for the slap/strum and back again. Slow this down to get the movements as small and precise as you can to increase your economy of motion.

Example 5j

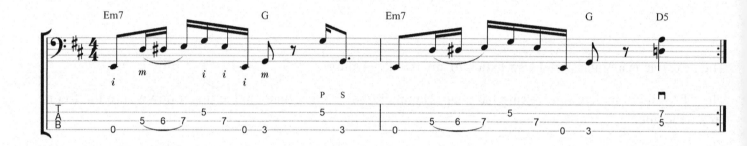

Tim Commerford

Rage Against The Machine riffs are bold statements that often use simple rhythms and notes. Example 5k uses the F# Minor Pentatonic scale which is great to use for funk rock riffs as you can access the open E string to create huge-sounding riffs.

Example 5k

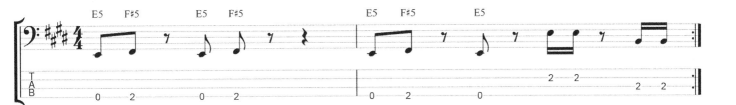

The blues scale is also common in RATM riffs. Use one finger (the second or third) to execute the slides at the end of bar two, then shift quickly back to the F# on the 2nd fret.

Write your own riffs in this key by using short F# Minor Pentatonic phrases with strong, simple rhythms.

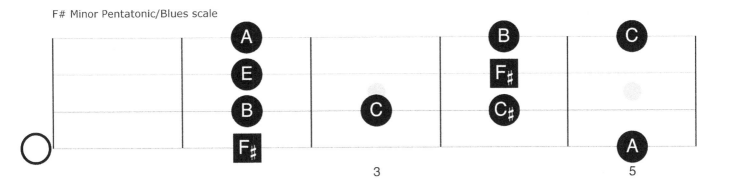

Example 5l

Hip Hop basslines were a huge influence on Commerford and many of his lines have a sample-like quality to them, based around repetitive infectious hooks. When you practice these riffs, think like a machine!

Unlike many of the grooves in this book, play this E Minor Blues riff exactly as written and don't add any fills. You need to be disciplined and precise when playing lines like this in a band because you could well be doubling the guitar part.

Example 5m

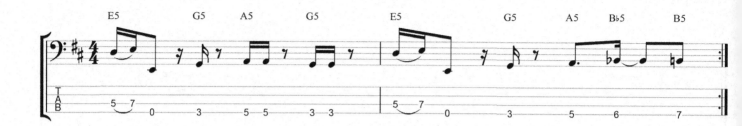

There is a subtle tonal difference between playing open string notes and fretting higher up the neck. Follow the TAB exactly as written below, but then try it using the open D and G strings in place of the 5th fret notes. See which you prefer.

Example 5n

The next riff is in drop D tuning. Tune your E string down a whole step and you're good to go. The pull-offs from the 5th to 3rd frets in bar two are quite difficult to play in time, so isolate them and practise the technique before trying the whole line. Drop D tuning is fun to explore, so get your fingers around the new shapes and get writing your own riffs.

Example 5o

Chapter Six – Slap

The players: Louis Johnson, Victor Wooten, Marcus Miller

Whole books have been written on slap bass and it is probably one of the main things people think of when it comes to Funk playing. This book shows that there's more to Funk than just slap, but it's so important that it deserves its own chapter here.

In the Early Funk chapter, we learnt that it was Larry Graham who popularised slap and that the purpose was to make the bass sound more percussive. The thumb slapping the strings mimics the kick drum and the middle or index finger pop mimics the snare.

Louis Johnson was a top session player and famous with his own group The Brothers Johnson. He played on *Thriller*, the best-selling album of all time, and was closely associated with Michael Jackson and Quincy Jones. They only called the best and Johnson got called a lot. Nicknamed "Thunder Thumbs" his style was aggressive and showy, with his hand often miles away from the fretboard. Many of his basslines created intense rhythms with the thumb, hence the moniker.

I remember the first time I ever saw Victor Wooten play live. Even though I'd heard him on videos before, it was still a shock to see that level of technical proficiency up close. As well as being a master educator (I highly recommend his book *The Music Lesson*) he pioneered the *double thumbing* technique in which the thumb is used like a plectrum to facilitate complex, fast playing with minimal movement.

Marcus Miller is another all-time great with a stellar solo career spanning decades. He's worked with a who's who of top musicians that include Miles Davis, Herbie Hancock and David Sanborn. He is equally as talented as a producer and film composer and produced many hits for Luther Vandross. A consummate professional and master musician, he is known for his expertise in many diverse roles.

His sound is unmistakable and a huge part of that is created by his slap technique where he excels at playing pure groove and hitting all the right notes.

Gear Checklist: Louis Johnson's trademark sound comes from the Music Man StingRay with its bright sound but fat, punchy tone. Johnson was one of the first to play the StringRay and certainly helped to popularise it.

Victor Wooten is associated with the New York high end bass manufacturer Fodera. His Yin Yang Monarch bass comes in various different specs, but he can be seen favouring one with a PJ pickup configuration, although also plays one with the more standard two jazz bass pickups.

He uses light gauge strings (40. 60. 80. 100.) which makes his pyrotechnics *slightly* easier to achieve. Wooten often used a hair tie to act as a mute when slapping, although Gruv Gear now make excellent fret wraps that do a brilliant job of taming open strings.

Marcus Miller got his signature tone by getting Roger Sadowsky to fit his '70s Fender Jazz with an active preamp to give him more high-end, and scope to shape his EQ. His sound is muscular with a low-end boost giving his slap sound a thunderous quality. He uses MarkBass amps and EBS pedals.

He has now helped develop the Sire bass range which are incredible value for money and many top pros use them. I highly recommend you check them out as the preamps are fantastic and the build quality is second-to-none in that price range.

Recommended Listening

Get on the Floor – Michael Jackson

Stomp! – The Brothers Johnson

Celebrations – The Brothers Johnson

U Can't Hold No Groove (If You Ain't Got No Pocket) – Victor Wooten

What Did He Say? – Victor Wooten (Live in America)

Funky D – Wooten, Chambers, Franceschini

Rio Funk – Lee Ritenour

Power – Marcus Miller

So Naughty – Chaka Khan

Louis Johnson

Slap playing requires a lot of fretting hand muting to keep notes short and reduce unwanted string noise. Example 6a requires you to focus on your muting technique and use any spare fingers to lightly dampen unplayed strings. You also need to dampen the open strings to keep them clean and short. Record yourself playing then listen back to let your ears be the judge of how much you need to mute. A recording never lies!

Example 6a

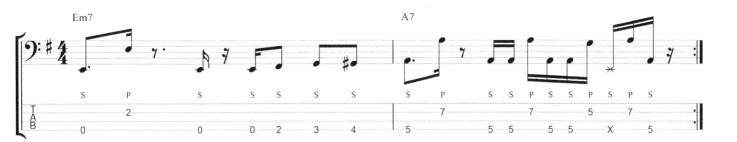

Louis Johnson was famous for slapping from a great height, but I think more of a Bruce Lee "one-inch punch" approach will help you here. Keep your slaps and pops as close to the fretboard as you can. This prevents your hand from jerking around too much and will increase your efficiency and accuracy.

Use the ghost notes to move your fretting hand lower down the neck.

Example 6b

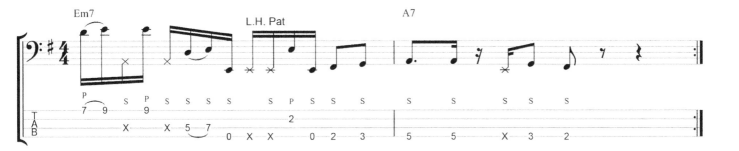

This next groove uses octave intervals to navigate through the chords. The pull-off at the end of bar two can be awkward to get in time, so isolate it and loop it slowly while tapping your foot.

There's a big jump from the G on fret 3 to the pull-off on the 9th. Use the fret markers to eyeball fret 9 so you can see exactly where you need to jump to in advance.

Example 6c

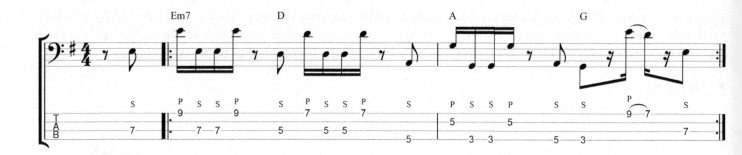

In Example 6d we follow a pop with a slap on the same note to create a cool percussive effect. This happens at the end of bar one on the F (3rd fret). At first it might be difficult to get your index finger then thumb to play on the same note, so isolate this section until you nail it.

Example 6d

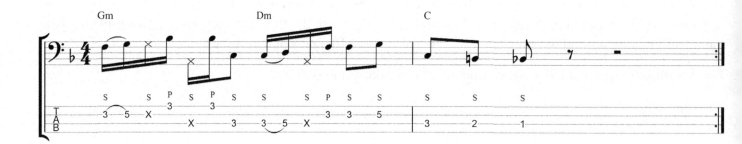

You can create long, steady streams of impressive 1/16th notes using interplay between your hands. Example 6e uses ghost notes and left-hand patting which is almost similar to tapping your hands on a table. Adding fretting hand articulations to this idea forms the basis of an advanced slap technique.

Play all the ghost notes in this example by patting the second and third fingers of your fretting hand against the open strings.

Example 6e

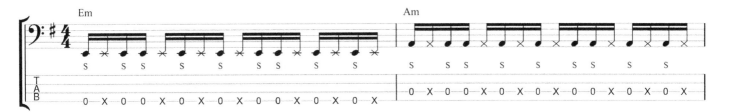

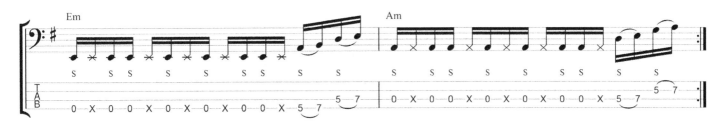

Victor Wooten

Example 6f showcases some of Wooten's one-man band techniques. He often plays lines that combine rhythm, harmony and melody in all registers. Play the high D on the 7th fret with your fourth finger and then quickly shift your hand as you slap the ghost note. It's a bit of a leap of faith but you can do it!

It doesn't matter where you fret this ghost note; just produce it while you're shifting your hand to the double-stops. Pop these with index and middle fingers.

Example 6f

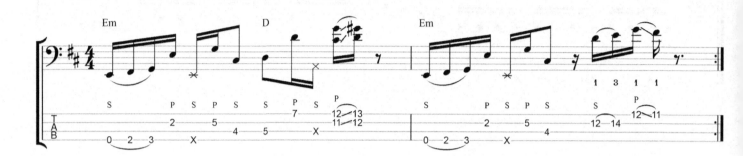

Wooten often uses more than one finger to pop consecutive notes, leading to faster playing, so be careful here to use your index and middle fingers as indicated. Aim to play those notes with consistent volume and speed between the fingers, and anchor your pinkie against the body to improve your accuracy.

Example 6g

Wooten is famous for pioneering the *double thumbing* technique, where the thumb is used like a plectrum with up and down strokes. This allows you to keep your hand in the same position and create a consistent tone. Allow your thumb to rest on the string below on the downstroke, then bring it back up, playing with the top of your thumb and thumbnail on the upstroke.

Practise this movement slowly as it's *very* awkward at first. Keep the thumb rigid and your wrist slightly more locked than normal as this will help things feel a bit steadier. Don't strain your wrist and if you feel any pain or discomfort then stop.

Don't worry if this technique feels alien, it's very specialised. If you want to get it down, be prepared to spend some months working on it!

Example 6h

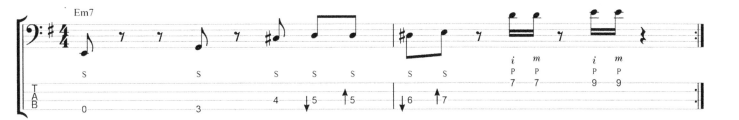

There are lots of tricks in Example 6i that include popping with the index and middle fingers, using left hand patting, hammer-ons from nowhere, and the use of 1/16th note triplets, so I've included a video lesson that breaks down the following complex groove. **https://geni.us/funkvideos**

The main feature is the rhythm created by the slap followed by a hammer-on-from-nowhere, followed by a pop which you can see in the first three notes. The rhythm created by that movement is the basis for the entire example. To practise it further you can play octaves up and down the neck or use scales in octaves.

Example 6i

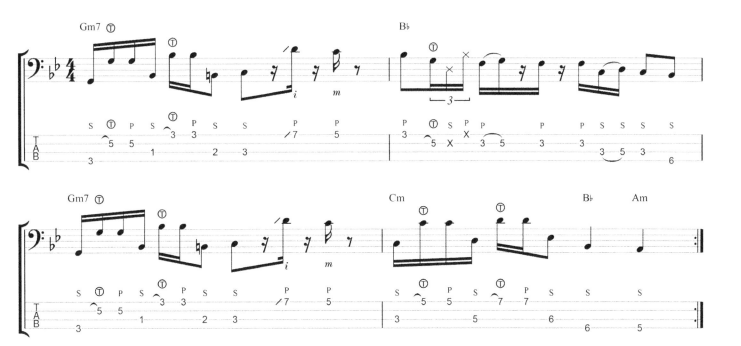

The melodic idea in the next groove uses slaps and pops, ghost notes, hammer-ons, pull-offs, and slides to create a fluid line. Notice how you can get lots of cool phrases by using two-string scale patterns; in this instance E Dorian on the D and G strings.

In bar two, use the hammer-on from the 5th to 7th fret to smoothly shift your hand across to the 7th and 9th. Anchor your pinkie finger against the body as you pop with your index and middle fingers.

Example 6j

Marcus Miller

Example 6k is in the key of A Minor and in the style of classic tune *Never Too Much*.

Stay tight and watch out for the pops at the end of the last bar which are easy to rush. You need to really focus on controlling the speed of your wrist as you slap. At the point your thumb strikes the E string, ensure your popping finger is *already* under the D string. That way, you simply lift up your index finger to play the note.

Example 6k

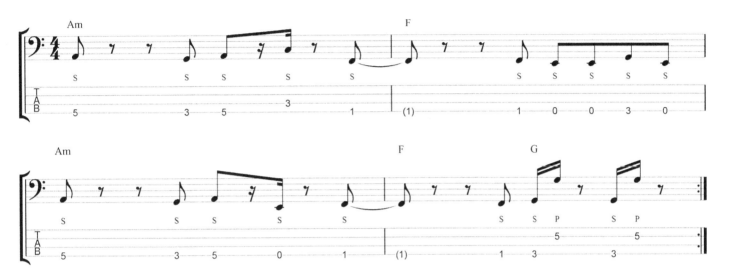

Don't be alarmed by the 1/32nd notes in Example 6l as the tempo is slow and they're not too hard to play. Listen to the audio example if you're in any doubt and keep your wrist super loose.

Remember, most of the slapping movement comes from the wrist and not your elbow or shoulder.

Example 6l

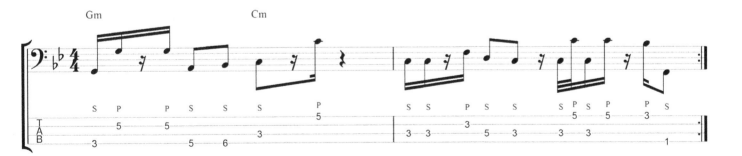

Miller loves to play fast rhythms in between his lines and end phrases with melodies. Example 6m uses both of these devices. His use of the thumb for this kind of playing is less technical than Victor Wooten's but very effective. Use your thumb as you normally would, except brush over the top the string a little like you would with a pick to ensure you're in position to carry on slapping.

Example 6m

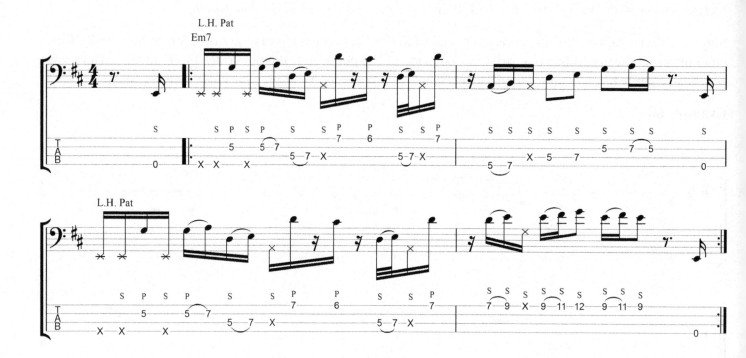

Simple lines with pop hooks create memorable basslines and one of the best is *Just the Two of Us* by Grover Washington Jr., featuring Bill Withers. Example 6n uses this as inspiration and combines octaves and movement through the E Natural Minor scale.

Example 6n

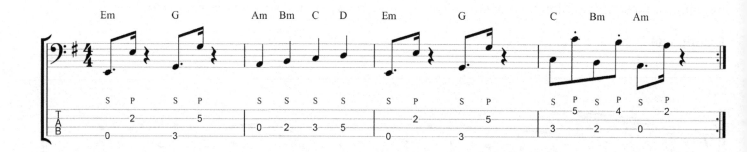

Example 6o is a cool line that uses just the thumb with some articulations, but the timing in your fretting hand is extremely important to create the overall feel. Slow down the first bar and focus on creating the rhythms with the hammer-ons, slide and pull-off.

Loop the drum backing track and try to add some fills over the last two beats using E Dorian.

Example 60

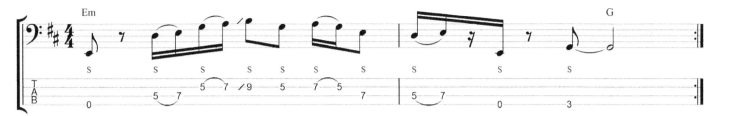

Chapter Seven – Funk Pop

The players: Jamiroquai, Prince, N.E.R.D.

In the 1980s, Pop artists and beyond started to add the raw power of Funk to their hook-based songs.

All the artists in this chapter are known more for their songs than for the genre they inhabit, but without the Funk there would have been no hits.

Jamiroquai's original line up included bassist Stuart Zender in their ranks before adding Nick Fyffe and the current incumbent, Paul Turner. The lead singer Jay Kay leans heavily on his fantastic band to channel old school Funk and Soul influences and this is a group that's always had the bass player at the forefront of the music.

Prince didn't care what you looked like, if you were funky and talented you could be in his band. Sonny Thompson, Andre Cymone, Andrew Gouché, Brown Mark, MonoNeon, Ida Nielson, Rhonda Smith and Nik West are all great bass players that worked with The Purple One.

Despite being a great bass player in his own right, Prince often didn't play it at all. But when he did, Funk played a big part.

N.E.R.D. blend many styles into their sound, including Hip Hop, RnB, EDM and rap. Pharrell Williams and Chad Hugo use various bass players, but normally come up with the basslines themselves. Often the bass parts are highly crafted and entire songs are built around them. *Hot-n-Fun* is a good example of this.

Gear Checklist: Stuart Zender's classic basslines were mostly recorded using a Warwick Streamer Stage 1 and later a Streamer Stage 2. Both basses have an ergonomic body and neck making them very comfortable to play. Paul Turner has loads of basses and pedals. His favourite bass is probably his 1966 Fender Jazz but currently he's endorsing Stenback basses.

Prince himself used many basses including Warwick and Fender Jazz. The many accomplished bassists who shared the stage with him say that he was obsessed with getting the right tone for the bass. Andrew Gouche, who played with him from 2011-14 once tried to get Prince to play his six-string bass. He refused and said, in a nod to one of his great influences, "Why you gotta have all those strings? Larry's [Graham] bass only has four strings!"

N.E.R.D.'s first and third albums featured Spymob as the backing band. Bassist Christian Twigg used a Fender Precision which helped contribute to the vintage sound Pharrell and Chad were after.

Recommended Listening
Time Won't Wait – Jamiroquai

Cosmic Girl – Jamiroquai

Love Foolosophy – Jamiroquai

Stare – Prince

Chelsea Rodgers – Prince

Black Muse – Prince

You Know What – N.E.R.D

Run to the Sun – N.E.R.D

Hot-n-Fun – N.E.R.D

Jamiroquai

All the Jamiroquai examples are in the key of C# Minor and played at 119 bpm so you can learn them individually and then move between them.

For the octaves in Example 7a, get your plucking hand middle finger ready for the higher note just before it's needed. So, when you pluck the first note on the A string with your index finger, your middle finger should *already* be in contact (or very close to) the G string. This will improve your timing no end.

Example 7a

Example 7b builds on the previous groove and adds two 1/16th notes to the higher octave.

Great basslines also contain great melodies and here's one that's built from the C# Minor Pentatonic scale.

You can always play simple octaves over a chord progression and connect the chords with the minor pentatonic scale to get some spectacular results. Use the patterns below to create your own lines and fills over this chord progression.

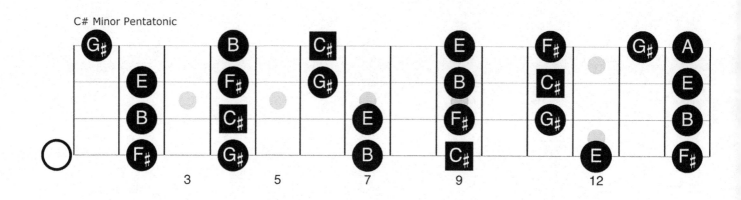

Example 7b

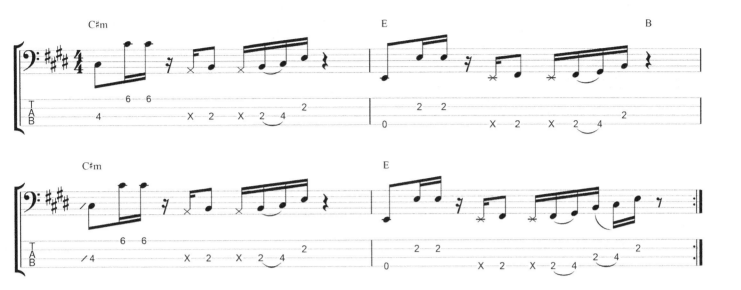

Not all Funk lines have to be flashy. Example 7c is a driving line using short, staccato quarter notes to propel the groove. Keep those notes even, on the beat, and take care not to rush. The fill in bar four is just a descending C# Minor Blues scale – an excellent scale for Funk fills.

Example 7c

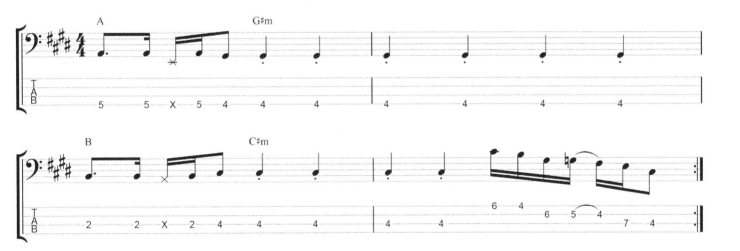

Knowing the notes that make up a chord is an essential skill that you should master.

A C# Minor arpeggio is outlined in bar one. Study the diagram below and then alter the order of notes you play in bars one and three. Focus on the funky rhythm and apply it to your note choices to practice improvising your own lines.

C# minor arpeggio

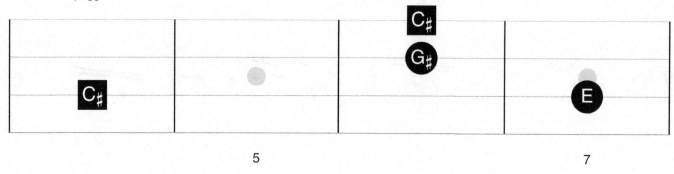

Example 7d

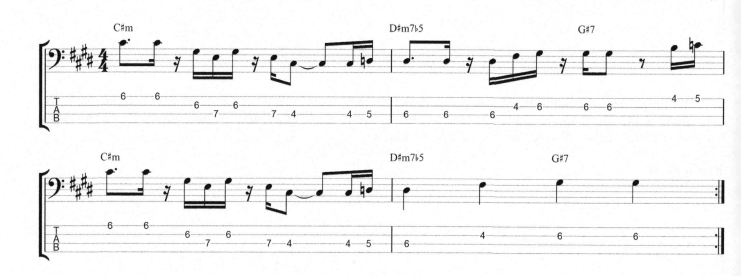

Controlling the length of the notes is very important in the next example. All the higher octave notes should be played as short as you can, and the tied notes held for their full length.

Run any of the drum backing tracks from these five examples and combine the examples in any order. Then try adding your own C# Minor Pentatonic fills.

Example 7e

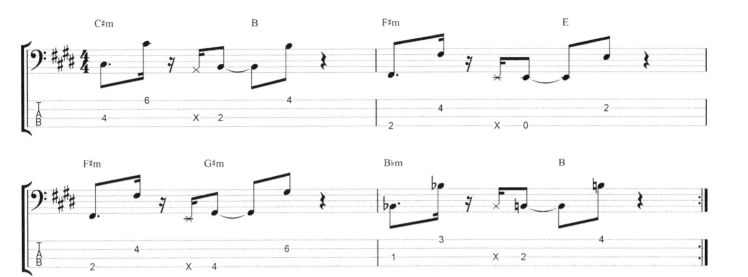

Prince

Example 7f is based around a G Mixolydian mode with added G Major Blues scale, which are both classic Funk scales. Follow the fingering patterns carefully as there are a few hand shifts required and it's much easier to avoid the open strings. Bend the last note a touch with your little finger.

Study the diagrams below. Along with the Dorian and Minor Blues scales, these two scales make up most of the Funk bass sounds you'll play. Memorise these patterns and add them to your own grooves.

G Mixolydian

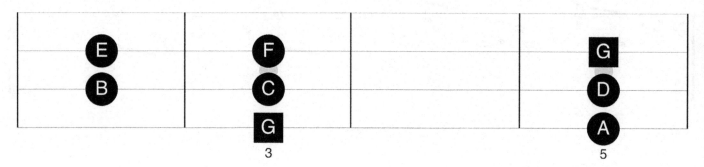

G Major Blues scale (the same as the G Major pentatonic with a flat third - Bb)

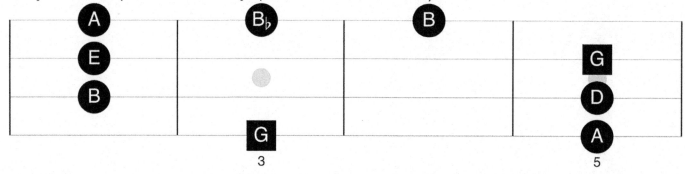

Example 7f

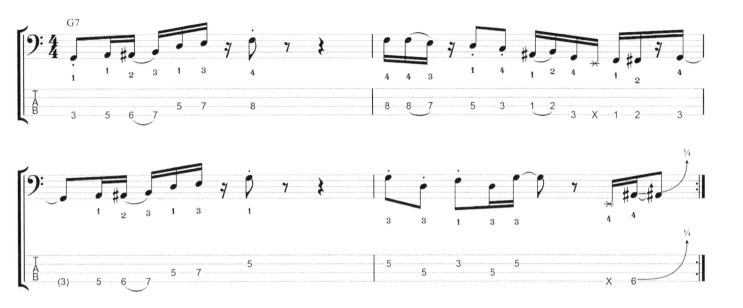

Space is very important in the next groove. The 1/8th notes in bar two are played short then long. You can alter the length of the notes with your plucking hand, catching the string you want to stop with the finger you're not using to pluck.

Example 7g

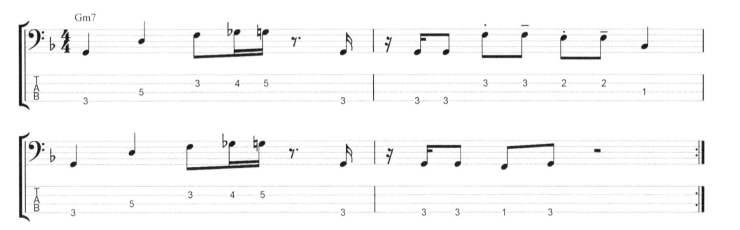

Chelsea Rodgers and *Black Muse* are both examples of Prince basslines that use octaves brilliantly. The key to these octave lines is to avoid having the low and high notes ringing into each other as this really gets in the way of the groove and is a huge Funk *faux pas*. Release pressure with your fretting hand finger to stop the note.

Example 7h

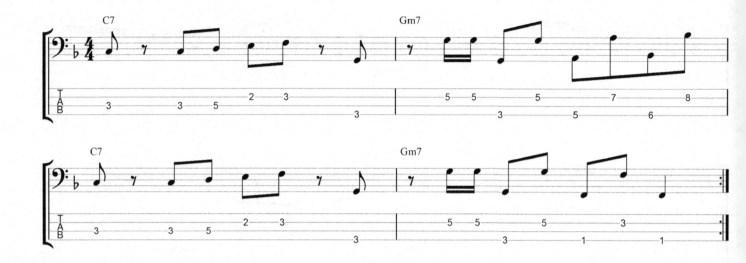

Sonny T had a flair for the flashy bassline and the next example is a fast, repetitive groove using ghost notes and 1/16ths to create excitement. Isolate the 1/16th notes as that section needs to be very precise. As always, slow it down and develop the coordination between the hands.

Example 7i

This example is in E Dorian and needs to be played aggressively. I've talked before about how a light touch is needed for some of the more complicated passages, but for this one you'll need to dig in hard.

Example 7j

N.E.R.D.

Example 7k starts with the hook. Slide to the A on the 7th fret with your little finger, then keep the rest of the line nice and punchy. Concentrate on counting the 1/16ths in beat one to keep the rhythm accurate and have some fun with the backing track.

Example 7k

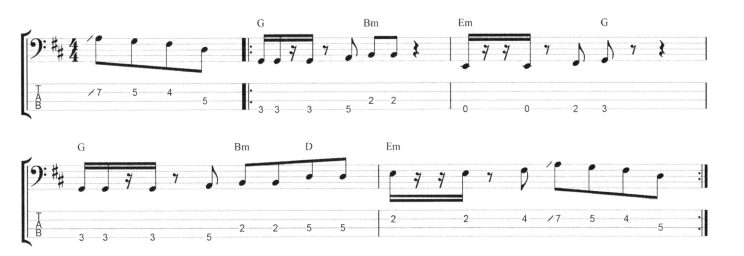

N.E.R.D. love to move from the iii to the IV chord (Em to F in the key of C Major) to create a Phrygian sound. It's a really modern, fresh sound that you can hear on *Like I Love You* by Justin Timberlake, and *She Wants to Move* by N.E.R.D. Example 7l uses the same chord progression.

Example 7l

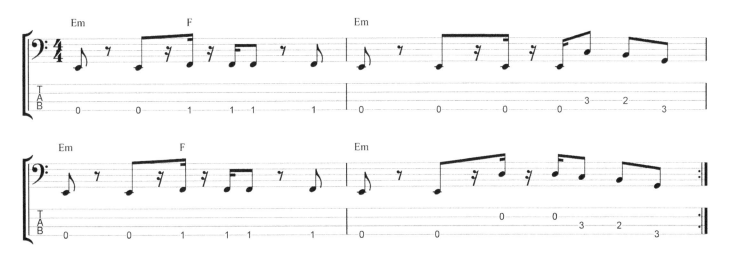

The following groove switches between very short notes and 1/4 notes held for their full length. In the final bar, fret the first three notes with your first, second, then third fingers before shifting up to play the next note with your first finger. That'll put you in position for the slide.

Example 7m

The next example uses more of the Mixolydian mode we explored earlier to create some melodic lines.

Check out the diagram below then concoct some melodic lines of your own.

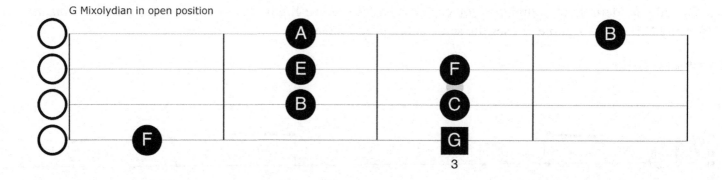

Example 7n

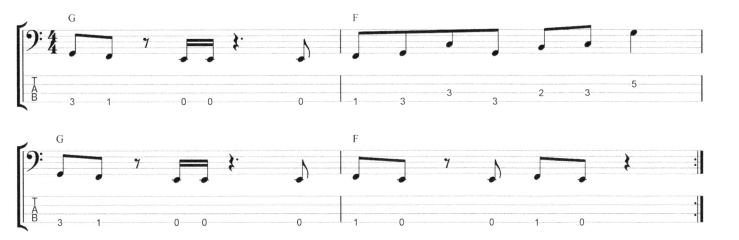

The final example in this book returns to the Phrygian tonality introduced in Example 7l. Play the entire line in second position and use the notes from the diagram below to add fills.

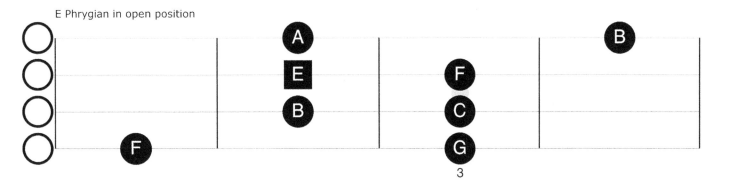

Example 7o

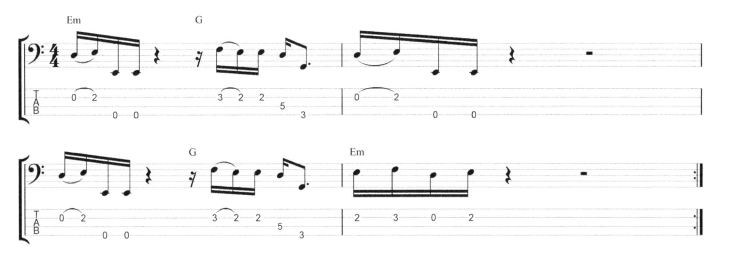

Chapter Eight – Resources

Tone Tips

I had many basses to choose from when recording the audio from this book, including a beautiful 1978 Music Man StingRay. In the end I plumped for my '75 Fender Jazz. Even though it has a slightly fatter neck than many Jazz basses, it plays fast and the original pickups nailed the muscular, piercing sound I was after.

The bass was plugged into an Avalon U5 and a handmade tube preamp, the Jule Monique. Very minimal EQ was added after the signal was recorded through a Universal Audio Apollo interface and into Logic. I blended both signals together to create a fat tone. Mixing two signals in this way creates an upfront, weighty tone that's perfect for Funk.

Funk often involves digging in hard or slapping and popping. Often this wide dynamic range needs to be evened out with a compressor and for this, I used a Cali 76 Compact bass pedal which is based on the famous Universal Audio 1176 outboard compressor.

Funk Pedalboard

Funk players only need a small pedalboard. Here are the effects on mine…

On my pedalboard:

- Compressor: Cali 76

- Preamp: Sadowsky (great for slap)

- Envelope filter: 3 Leaf Audio Proton

- Overdrive: Darkglass Vintage Microtubes

- Fuzz: Pro Co The Rat

- Line 6 M5 (chorus, delays, filters, and more)

- Bananana Effects Matryoshka (synth pedal)

I put all my pedals in loops using a Brightonion true bypass looper pedal. This avoids any signal degradation I might get when chaining multiple units, which can suck out the tone. Also, when you're shopping, look for pedals that have a mix or blend knob as this will allow you to keep the bottom end of your bass signal. And obviously avoid any pedals that cut out bottom end!

Here are some famous funk pedals to consider, all listed with a cheaper or more modern alternative. Don't get too hung up on brands because gear nowadays is of an incredible standard, so most pedals are high quality and will sound good. Go for bass specific pedals that have a blend function (to retain your low end) or consider placing your pedals in loops (such as from a Brightonion or The Gig Rig Quartermaster).

There are also pedals that allow you to blend your original signal with the wet/effected sound. The This1smyne blender is excellent for that job.

Original Funk Pedal	Alternative
Mu-Tron III (envelope filter)	Aguilar Filter Twin
Akai Deep Synth	Future Impact I
Maestro PS-1 Phase Shifter	MXR Phase 90
Boss OC-2 (Octave pedal. The '80s ones sound great)	EBS OctaBass
Ibanez C9 (chorus)	Boss CEB-3
Electro Harmonix Big Muff	Source Audio Aftershock
MXR Dyna Comp (compressor)	Origin Effects Cali 76

Further Listening

I hope that this book has shown you that there are many different flavours of Funk and given you some great grooves to play. I'm sure you already have your favourites! Keep learning and listening and you will discover your voice as you explore. Figure out as much as you can by ear and listen out for common patterns, sounds and scales. You'll have noticed many common themes in this book, but the real magic happens when you can make those connections on your own. It all comes down to the most important thing you can do as a musician: *listen*.

My included Spotify playlist contains over twelve hours of Funk classics:

Here are a few essentials…

Bass Player	Band	Song
Nate Phillips	Pleasure	*Glide*
George Porter Jr.	The Meters	*Cissy Strut*
Robert 'Kool' Bell	Kool & The Gang	*Jungle Boogie*
Larry La Bes	Fat Larry's Band	*Act Like You Know*
John Taylor	Duran Duran	*Girls on Film*
Janice-Marie Johnson	A Taste of Honey	*Boogie Oogie Oogie*
Wes Stephenson	Mark Lettieri	*Naptime*
Anthony Jackson	The O'Jays	*For the Love of Money*
Michael Henderson	Miles Davis	*One and One*
Ida Nielsen	Ida Nielsen	*Throwback*
Will Lee	The Brecker Brothers	*Some Skunk Funk*
Trevor Dunn	Mr. Bungle	*Squeeze Me Macaroni*
Alan Gorrie	Average White Band	*Let's Go Round Again*
Nate Watts	Stevie Wonder	*I Wish*
Chuck Rainey	Aretha Franklin	*Rock Steady*
Robbie Shakespeare	Grace Jones	*Pull Up to The Bumper*
Stanley Clarke	Stanley Clarke	*We Supply*
Mark King	Level 42	*Mr. Pink*
Jamareo Artis	Bruno Mars	*Uptown Funk*

Next Steps

I wrote this book not only to teach you different styles of Funk, but also to help you learn about its main characters and colourful history. However, it's a massive genre and I feel that I've only just scratched the surface. Use the further listening list as a springboard for your own journey down the funky rabbit hole.

I've tried to give you an insight into how the examples were written and taught you how a handful of scales, techniques, and rhythms open up a whole world of possibilities. You should use the ideas here to spur your own creativity and start writing your own lines, fills and melodies right away. Use the scales and arpeggios to jam, connect the dots and *create*! The more you do this the better you'll get, and this is true in any style.

The best way to improve your Funk playing is by playing with other musicians – especially great drummers. Find as many as you can and play with them regularly. Your timing will tighten, your groove will soar, and your pocket will deepen.

I release weekly free bass lessons and tips at **www.onlinebasscourses.com** as well as offering courses and other resources. I'd love to see you over there.

Good luck and stay funky!

Dan

P.S. If you've enjoyed this book, I'd be eternally grateful if you could leave a warm review on Amazon. That really helps me as an author, and will help other bass players around the world to get the Funk!

Connect with Dan

Instagram: **OnlineBassCourses**

YouTube: **OnlineBassCourses**

Made in the USA
Las Vegas, NV
11 September 2021